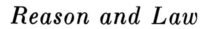

Reason and Law

REASON
and LAW

STUDIES IN JURISTIC PHILOSOPHY

by MORRIS RAPHAEL COHEN

THE FREE PRESS, GLENCOE, ILLINOIS

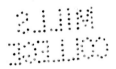

PRINTED IN THE UNITED STATES OF AMERICA
BY THE MODERN FRANKLIN CO., CHICAGO, ILL.

Table of Contents

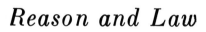

Reason and Law

Prologue:
My Philosophy of Law

The philosophy of any special subject-matter, such as the law, I take to be the effort to view it as part of a larger whole wherein it moves and has its being. From this point of view no hard and fast line separates the philosophy from the science or theory of law,— the distinction between them can only be one of the degree of generality of our interest.

Though professional legal writings are naturally dominated by practical and technical issues, the great jurists have always drawn directly or indirectly on what philosophers such as Aristotle, Aquinas, Leibniz, Kant, and Hegel have written on the law. It is only in the last century that philosophy almost entirely ceased to pay attention to the nature of legal institutions and other historic realities, and became absorbed in the psychologic or epistemologic problem of how we come to know anything at all. On the other hand, the distrust, if not contempt, for jurisprudence or abstract legal theory has been strongest among English and American lawyers, largely because of the narrowly professional character of our law schools. The growing annexation of the latter by our universities tends to make law teachers aim at being scholars rather than mere practitioners, and this promotes a more liberal interest in legal theory. Unfortunately, relatively few teachers of law have had a scientific education, and so their conception of scientific method does not always rise above popular impressions.

One of the most widespread of these misimpressions is that philosophy proceeds deductively from intuitive or *a priori* first principles, while science proceeds inductively from an examination of the facts. Though this distinction is often asserted by scientists when they leave their work and begin to philosophize, it is clearly untenable at either end. (a) No science can be entirely inductive, and (b) if philosophy were purely deductive it would, like pure mathematics, be entirely

Reprinted by permission of the West Publishing Company from *My Philosophy of Law* (Boston Law Book Company), Copyright, 1941.

1

hypothetical[1] and could not assert anything about law or indeed about any specific form of existence such as mind or nature.

(a) It is easy to say: Begin with the observation of the facts. But what the facts are is far from being clear or self-evident to the naked or untrained eye. Indeed, to find all the relevant facts is the final goal of the carefully elaborated procedure which we call scientific method. But discoveries in science are made only by those who know what to look for, and to do this we must have some preliminary ideas as to the way things are connected. Furthermore, the meaning of anything we discover depends on the context in which it is placed.

(b) On the other hand, exact logic shows the impossibility of deducing any particular fact from purely universal principles alone. You cannot, for instance, deduce the path of any planet from the laws of gravitation and general mechanics without additional premises in regard to its shape, its distance from the sun, and its mass as compared with the latter. And it ought to be even more obvious that the decision of the legal cases or the determination of concrete legal issues cannot be deduced from principles alone but must involve also assumptions of fact. Moreover, the distinction between facts and principles is unfortunately less clear in the legal than in the physical realm, as witnessed by the general difficulty of distinguishing clearly between the function of the judge and that of the jury, or by the many difficulties of the New York Code which requires a complaint to confine itself to a statement of the facts of the case.

What is law? If we recognize that a definition is a resolution to use a word in a certain sense, we need not argue as to which is *the* proper definition of law; we may only ask whether any given definition is consistently followed and whether the meaning of the word used is always clearly indicated. And if we view definitions as attempts to state briefly the essential nature of any actual or historic object such as the law, we must recognize that a diversity of such definitions is possible because different writers are concerned about different parts or aspects of it. Only when one denies a material proposition that someone else affirms do we have real contradiction.

These considerations should help us to clarify the controversy

---

[1] It is now fairly established that rigorous deduction rather than restriction to traditional number or quantity is the essence of pure mathematics, and hence every strict science must have a mathematical element.

between those who emphasize the existential aspect of the law and those who stress its normative character.

Actuated perhaps by the fact that in the natural sciences the word *law* denotes an invariant uniformity of phenomena and by the popular (but quite erroneous) notion that science can deal only with actual existences, extreme positivists insist that a science of the law can deal only with the uniformities of actual behavior either of the people generally or of officials such as judges and administrators. This tends to identify law with prevailing custom, and the implicit ideal of the science of law is that of a branch of sociology as a natural science. The opponents of this view emphasize the fact that law is imperative or prescriptive of what men should do rather than descriptive of what they in fact do. The factual violation of a statutory or common-law rule does not impair its validity. The model of normative science is thus pure logic so far as the latter is a science of what should be inferred from given propositions rather than of what all or even most men do infer.

As in so many other disputes each side here emphasizes a part to the neglect, and sometimes, alas, to the explicit denial, of the rest of the truth.

It is certainly worthwhile to study what Ehrlich has called "living law," that is, the actual ways in which people such as Slovene or Ruthenian peasants conduct their affairs. And we may extend that term also to what juristically advanced peoples (who follow legislative enactments and judicial decisions) assume the law of their country to be. What is disputed, however, is whether it is humanly possible to banish the evaluational point of view from an adequate science of the law. Certainly those who have opposed all natural law or normative jurisprudence have not always been free of crypto-idealism, that is, of implicitly assuming some ideal of what the law should be, often some idealization of the *status quo*. The objection to such procedure is that the values thus tacitly assumed escape the critical consideration that distinguishes scientific procedure from dogmatism.

We cannot logically identify the 'legal' simply with what men actually do. For the same physical act can be legal or illegal, and which it shall be depends upon the logical consequences of the statutory or judicial rule applied to it. Certainly, when an honest

judge wishes to determine what is the law in a given case, he is looking for a principle (or an analogous case embodying one) to guide
him as to how he *should* rule and not to predict how he will rule.
Indeed, such questions as "Who is a judge?" and "When is one acting in a judicial capacity?" cannot be answered by any statement of
physical facts. The answers to such questions depend upon the
validity of certain claims.

It is to the credit of Kelsen and his followers that they have insisted
on the distinction between social fact and legal validity. But they
create insuperable difficulties when they draw a sharp dichotomy
between mind or spirit and nature, and try to envisage the law as
outside or independent of the latter. The law is not a homeless,
wandering ghost. It is a phase of human life located in time and
space. Human beings outside of nature are not the objects of science.

The legal system of any country has a definite history which helps
us to understand its provisions and shows how it changes according
to varying social conditions, and even according to the will of certain
powerful individuals. And this in no way denies that without logical
connections there could be no legal order or system. Though the law
may never become a completely logical system, it can never entirely
dispense with the effort in that direction. For that helps men to
know what they may or may not do.

This way of viewing the logical and the existential as polar com-
plementaries enables us to clarify an old and persistent controversy
as to whether the law is or is not a closed system. Against the latter
view it has been urged that no actual set of rules devised by any
human agency can possibly foresee all contingencies and make provision for dealing with them, and hence that the judge who has to
decide all the cases that come before him must necessarily legislate and
thus fill the gaps or incompletenesses in the existing law. I have, myself,
repeatedly urged this and still do. Nevertheless, we may distinguish
between formal and material completeness. Thus, while the system of
natural science is constantly changing through the assimilation of new
information, it may be regarded as logically or formally complete
because all the changes in it are made in accordance with the principles
immanent in it. Science is a complete system in so far as it is self-
corrective. Similarly, any legal system such as that of the American
Constitution can be said to be complete if legislation or amendments

to it are made in accordance with its provisions.

Another objection to viewing the law as a complete system regulating all social contact is based on the fact that every legal system contains, besides orders and prohibitions, many explicit and more implicit provisions that are permissive, so that even the most despotic government does and must leave a great deal unregulated, and thus allow liberty of free choice on the part of individuals. But while this is perfectly true, it is well to note that our liberty or freedom within the law to do what we want would be null if it were not effectively protected by prohibiting everyone else from interfering with such liberty. My freedom to go to a concert or not depends on the protection which I receive in choosing either alternative, and thus on the law that restrains others from interfering. Thus, the absence of law in cases of liberty is only apparent. Liberties or privileges are part of the whole legal system.

This is not a merely verbal matter. Its realization cuts the ground from the anarchistic error that all law is restraint on freedom, so that the less legislation, the more men are free. Legislation makes a change within the legal system; and if it takes away the liberty of some, it thereby creates liberties for others. Whether the total result is good or bad must be determined by an analysis of all the actual consequences and not by the mere fact that there has been legislation.

We can similarly see the error of those who minimize the social importance of the law enforced by the courts. They argue that only the exceptional or marginal transaction terminates in litigation. But this ignores the fact that the decisions of courts do directly or indirectly become guides to what men may or may not undertake in all similar cases.

We may summarize the foregoing by considering Holmes's much-cited dictum that "the life of the law has not been logic, it has been experience." Obviously, the truth of this as of other neat dicta depends on the meaning we attach to the words in it.

Whatever the meaning of the word 'life', no one identifies it with pure logic. But if logic denotes the tracing of the necessary implication and thus the clarification of our statements, it should be equally clear that the life of the law is not the kind of experience that can dispense with all logic and consistency. Once we get rid of the false assumption that experience and logic are mutually exclusive, we can express the precise truth of our dictum by saying that logic is necessary but not by itself sufficient for the human experience we call law.

What the objectors to logic in the law seem to have in mind is really the narrow hard-heartedness of those who in the name of logic or consistency cling to some legal rule or maxim as a premise without being willing to see its limitations, or the need of its being supplemented by other premises called for by a more sympathetic understanding of the actual situation. We must also remember that under the word "logic," many understand certain aesthetic considerations, intellectual symmetries, or *elegantia juris,* which appeal more to the professional jurist than to those whose lives are thereby materially affected.

Though most of us profess to esteem logical accuracy and clarity very highly, there are basic human needs opposed to them. There are in the first place unpleasant truths from which we turn away our minds almost as instinctively as we cover our eyes or turn away our heads from too strong a light or from a horrible sight. And when we cannot but admit such truths, we do not like to speak of them except through euphemisms. This is a fruitful source of legal fictions. Then, again, language is not only a means of conveying truths,—its scope would notably contract if that were the case,—but it is also a part of social conduct. Just as there are conventionally prescribed ceremonial forms in regard to social intercourse, so there are rules of decorum in regard to linguistic expression. In Japan every victory of the army or navy must be attributed to the virtue of the Emperor; in England every law,—and indeed every national act—is due to the pleasure of his Majesty; and in the United States the judiciary is always independent, and whatever it decides follows from the Constitution. Even one who knows that these statements are not literally true, finds it difficult to avoid such expressions. In any case, these conventional fictions obscure the truth, especially in confusing what we wish to believe with what is actually the case.

While logic helps us to see the inadequacies of existing rules and the possibility of varying them or departing from them, it cannot by itself determine what new premises are necessary to make the law work more satisfactorily or to satisfy the maximum of human needs. When we ask: how are we to choose the basic premises of our legal system we enter the realm of ethics as the science of ultimate human ends. And since the law is imperative, it is well to remember that by no logical legerdemain can we get a *should* or *ought* into our conclusion unless we have one in our premises. But the principle of polarity should help us to avoid both the identification of law with justice and also their complete divorce. To say that the law is always just is to do violence to the fact that all sorts of outrageous villains and villainies have prospered under it, while some of our noblest heroes have had to revolt against it. That in the long run justice will triumph in the law is a matter of faith, not of knowledge. It will certainly not occur so long as men lack complete knowledge and perfect good will.

On the other hand, every legal system does embody some element of justice. For no integrated social action is possible without some adjustment among the different elements that co-operate. No matter how vicious and sadistic a governing group may be, it is to its interest that the governed prosper so as to be able to pay taxes or supply other revenues. Moreover, so large a role does inertia or social heredity play in the law, as in other realms, that the most absolute despot cannot always change it to suit his evil disposition.

In discussing the relation of law to justice it is well to distinguish between the formal and the material, between justice before the law and justice in the law. The classical maxim, "Justice is giving everyone his due", is applicable to legal procedure, where it means that the judge or administering officials should be impartial, i.e., honestly follow the law and not extend favors or disfavors to those who are not legally entitled to them. But the content of laws thus scrupulously obeyed may itself be most unjust. The bitter cry for justice on the part of the legally oppressed throughout the ages ought not to be ignored.

This is not the place for a discussion of the content of material justice. But it is well to be warned against seemingly self-evident principles such as that all men are equal, that every man is entitled to the products of his labor, and the like. A critical examination of these shows them to be either too vague to give us determinate results, or else productive of repellant consequences when strictly applied. It is also well to note the superior wisdom of the law (as against abstract moralists) in recognizing the claim of custom or the *status quo* as such. The latter create expectations, and to shock or defeat them is to effect an evil justified only if a greater evil can thereby be avoided. We must also get rid of the snobbishly sentimental idea that the high dignity of the law is contaminated if it is too much concerned with material economic interests. Even religion cannot ignore man's need for his daily bread. But while common economic interests form one of the strongest bonds which unite people into community or state, it is foolish to ignore the fact that they also divide us into conflicting or competitive groups. Increased revenue for the landed nobility does not always promote that of their tenants. Nor are increased profits and increased wages always compatible. And while rebel aristocrats sometimes espouse the cause of the poor, most human beings see the issues of economic justice from the point of view of the class in which they were born or with which they have been long associated. Thus, laborers identify their interests with those of the people, the middle classes with those of the public, and the wealthier classes with those of the country. But the very existence of class conflicts belies the theory that any one class is so omnipotent that the law merely registers its will. While some classes are doubtless more powerful than others, the law generally represents a compromise very much like a peace treaty. And, in general, legal order depends more on respect for the law and even on the need to be ruled than on mere brute force. And as people become enlightened and critical, the legal order can prevail against violations of it through fraud, criminal violence, or rebellion, only to the extent that it promotes a maximum attainable satisfaction to all groups.

No discussion of the philosophy of law can properly omit reference to the ultimate aims of the law and the extent to which it can influence human fate. Are human values commensurable, i. e., is there a common unit so that we may determine the relative claims on the law of aesthetic, religious, economic, and other social interests? What can or may the law achieve, and what is beyond its power or proper domain? What reality can we assign to the will of groups or of the state and to what extent are ideals effective in moulding the law?

But the limitations of space, like death, are not conducive to a rational development and ending.

CHAPTER ONE

Legal Philosophy in the Americas

1. THE BACKGROUND

A S THE BACKGROUND of legal philosophy in the Americas I take the general ideas that the European settlers brought with them and that have continued to influence the subsequent development of their legal systems.

At first glance, practitioners are impressed with the fact that the modes of legal thought brought to Latin America were quite different from those of Anglo-Saxon lands. The law of the former was Roman in origin and was developed first by the classical jurists and subsequently by university teachers, who, up to recently, were theologians; while the English common law originated in feudal litigation in the King's Court, and was elaborated by a body of professional practitioners organized in the Inns of Court, independent of the universities and of any particular philosophic school. On closer examination, however, it becomes evident that despite these and other radical differences, the fundamental ideas of the two systems have common origins in the classical Græco-Roman conceptions of law, in Christian thought, and in feudalism, and that these ideas have persisted despite the Reformation, subsequent wars, and different economic and political developments.

Scholars hardly need to be reminded that as late as the first half of the sixteenth century, English common law was Norman-French, not only in language, but also in its organization and largely in substance. The chief law officer of the realm, the Chancellor, was usually a cleric, and he and his clerks or clerics were generally familiar with Romanized canon law.

The extent to which Roman Law infiltrated into medieval England can be seen in the fact that no one regarded it as improper for

---

A paper read at the Eighth American Scientific Congress (1940) and published in the Proceedings thereof, Vol. 10, p. 501 (U. S. Department of State, 1943).

Bracton to embody pages of Azo into his account of English Law. The main incidence of feudal law and the rights of towns found similar development in all the western European countries. Nor is it necessary to recount the common origin of our commercial law governing not only our equity procedure but also bills and notes, admiralty, and the like. The mere mention of the laws of Rhodes, of Oleron, or the *Consolato del Mar* (formulated in Barcelona) is sufficient. But it is well to be reminded that despite popular myths to the contrary, the Reformation did not completely break up the intellectual community of Western Civilization as envisaged by men like Dante or Erasmus. To this common civilization, pagan philosophers such as Plato, Aristotle, Cicero, and Seneca, as well as the Bible, the Christian fathers such as St. Augustine, and the doctors of the medieval universities such as St. Thomas, all contributed. A striking illustration of this truth is afforded us by Perry Miller's book on *The New England Mind,* showing how strong that tradition and even the substance of St. Thomas' philosophy was in our Puritan colonies in the seventeenth century. It is true that modern science and philosophy found earlier acceptance in English-speaking colleges than in Spanish and Portuguese universities, and that consequent contempt for medieval scholastic philosophers became fashionable in the former. But without minimizing that important fact, it is well not to exaggerate its effects. The substance of scholastic philosophy can be found in the writings of Samuel Johnson, the president of King's College, later Columbia University, and in the Scottish philosophy of common sense which dominated American education up to the end of the nineteenth century. Certainly in the field of international law the common tradition of all the Americas goes back to the teaching of Vitoria at Salamanca and Suárez at Coimbra as well as Alberico Gentili at Oxford, and the more English, though no less scholastic, John Selden.

It is true that since the seventeenth century, English writers have more freely invoked Grotius and his successors, to the relative neglect of the Dominican and Jesuit theologians who had developed modern international law for the leading European nation in the sixteenth century, namely, Spain. But apart from the fact that Grotius was a Protestant rather than a Catholic theologian, the substance of his work continued that of Vitoria and Suárez, and he freely acknowledged his debt. This is important not only for the consideration of international law but for jurisprudence generally. For the idea of natural law as expounded by Grotius spread in England (through men such as Herbert of Cherbury, Rutherforth, and Cumberland), so that they became commonplaces (see, e.g., Blackstone's *Commentaries*). And even in the nineteenth century when Whewell came to write his *Elements of Morality*, he had Grotius and Puffendorf before him. But while professional English lawyers were somewhat insular in their conservatism and did not welcome changes urged on the authority of natural rights, even when pressed by the great Chief Justice Mansfield, doctrines of natural law and natural rights ruled in the American colonies, molded the Declaration of Independence and Bill of Rights, and have continued to dominate our theories of fundamental law and the Constitution. Our publicists and constitutional lawyers, to be sure, appealed rather to Locke and Sydney, to Montesquieu, Vattel, and Burlamaqui than to the Spanish jurist-theologians. But their ideas went back to a common source in Aristotle, Isocrates, the Stoics, and the classical jurists as elaborated by St. Thomas and other scholastic theologians. Nor need this surprise us when we remember that St. Thomas has been referred to as the first Whig, that the Dominican Order introduced representative government in its constitution, and that Vitoria defined the rights of the American Indians against both Pope and Emperor. And while the Jesuits completely subordinated the individual to the church, they were, as defenders of the Papacy, vigorous opponents of the doctrine of the Divine Right of Kings, and often went far in insisting that ultimate political power belongs to the whole community.

2. THE DISTINCTIVE DEVELOPMENT

To these indications of the common background of legal philosophy in America, we should add a fact which distinguished those who came here from Spain and Portugal, and which, in addition to the distinctive physical and ethnic conditions which they encountered, powerfully influenced the development of the Latin American attitude to law. I refer to the Crusades which began hundreds of years earlier in the Iberian Peninsula than they did in the rest of Europe, and, in the form of the African wars, lasted well into the sixteenth century. Indeed, the conquest of America was in some respects a continuation of the wars against the Mohammedans and Moors. The crusading wars gave the military caste and the clergy a power and prestige that

definitely affected the general valuation of the legal order. Thus, the
Inquisition not only suppressed free inquiry and the development of
new ideas, but in its methods of torture, and in denying to those sus-
pected of heresy the right of being speedily brought to an open trial
or even to be informed of the charges against them, there was a
systematic disregard of that respect for human personality that is
essential to any legal procedure that can be generally regarded as
just or fair.

On the other hand, the sanctification of war and the continuous
support of a military class led to a contempt for the values of industry
and commerce and to the honoring of the ready resort to arms in the
form of military rebellions that were profoundly inimical to the deliberate settlement of issues by peaceful legal procedure. It is only in
very recent times that the constructive work of men like Andrés Bello,
Juárez, and Sarmiento towards orderly legal development has been
duly honored by their people.

Not unrelated to the foregoing is the initial difference in the political
status between the settlers of Latin America and those who settled in
the English or Dutch colonies. The latter came from countries where
the power of the kind or prince was limited, and colonists retained their
rights as English or Dutch. The Latin American colonies were not
strictly under Spain or Portugal, but only under their respective kings
who governed through a hierarchy of officials without any cooperation
or check from the American population.

To the foregoing we must add the equally important fact that those
who came from Spain and Portugal found entirely different conditions
confronting them than did the English settlers. The former came as
conquerors of a country that was fairly well settled and integrated
politically, and though there was considerable intermarriage, the conquerors remained a ruling caste, ruling over the natives whom they
regarded as inherently inferior, so that to enslave them seemed quite
natural. The English came as communities to continue in the new
land the general kind of life they led in the old. The Indians they met
were seldom agriculturists, had no cities, and were readily pushed back
as the white population expanded, because of its better organization,
more intensive cultivation of the soil, and its commerce with the Old
World. The English colonists continued to be self-governing in their
local affairs, and the diversities of religion in New England, New York,

Pennsylvania, and the South prevented an encrustation of views in regard to the claims of established institutions.

Colonists seldom exceed the achievements of their mother country during the first few generations, and both Spain and Portugal suffered considerable cultural decline after the reign of Philip the Second. Even in the field of theology, let alone the modern sciences, the seventeenth and eighteenth centuries failed to match the achievements of the previous age. Moreover, the restrictions on commerce, even among the colonists themselves, isolated the latter from the great streams of European thought. And the censorship of the Inquisition prevented access to any new movements in thought. Even Adam Smith's *Wealth of Nations* was condemned. But the new learning, which had first appeared in Italy, began to make its way through France into Latin America in the latter part of the eighteenth century, especially after the more liberal commercial laws of 1778 made visits of wealthy creoles to France more frequent. Thus, through his tutor, Rodríguez, and through his own travels, Bolívar became acquainted not only with the writings of Montesquieu, Rousseau, Holbach, and Helvétius, but also with those of Hobbes, Spinoza, Hume, and Bentham. In the period which may be called the Age of Enlightened Despots, i.e., that of Charles the Third and Joseph the First (through his minister-dictator, Pombal), the universities were somewhat liberalized and secular subjects began to be added to the old curriculum of Latin, Medieval Philosophy, and Theology. The American and French Revolutions naturally stirred men's minds. Paine's *Rights of Man* was translated by Narino, and seems to have been widely circulated despite suppression by the Inquisition. The wars of liberation logically involved the elimination of slavery, and a general liberalization of the rights of man and of citizens. Many features of the United States Constitution were embodied in the fundamental laws of the Spanish American countries, and the ideal of international peace fired men's minds. But, as a result of the civil wars and brutal dictatorships which followed the wars of independence, there was naturally an intellectual reaction. Even the great liberator, Bolívar, began to be afraid of the effect of new studies on the minds of the youth, and ordered the universities to go back to more courses on Church history and canon law. This reaction, however, did not prove to be permanent. The influence of the various schools of legal philosophy in Europe, German historicism, French positivism, the English utilitarianism of Bentham, and especially the idealistic organic view of Krause, made their way into Spain and into the leading Latin American universities. More recently, the various forms of Neo-Kantian and Neo-Hegelian philosophy have been crowding the positivistic, sociologic views of law. In any case, these institutions are now quite secular and cosmopolitan, but they continue in the medieval tradition to the extent that law is taught not merely to train lawyers for private practice but as a part of wisdom in regard to the public regulation of human affairs in their political and social-economic aspects.

In regard to the development of legal philosophy in the United States, only a few words must suffice.

Though Scotch, Dutch, German, French Huguenot and other European peoples with the tradition of Roman law have shared in molding the ethos of the United States, and though elements of French and Spanish law still persist in some of our states, our legal system has remained basically English in the field of private law, though modified by our freer land economy.

In the latter part of the eighteenth and the early years of the nineteenth century, hostility to England gave great vogue to the French and Dutch writings on jurisprudence and civil law. This fashion, however, soon disappeared. Our democratic communities regarded the practice of law as a business, and were jealous of educational requirements. Until recently most of our lawyers acquired their training as clerks to practitioners, supplemented in earlier days by reading Coke, and after 1770 Blackstone. Our few law schools originally had no, or only a financial, connection with our colleges. Even now hardly any of them teach the general science of law, comparative jurisprudence, or even the history of American law. Still the general currents of thought have not left our jurisprudence untouched.

Manchester individualism and Spencer's *Social Statics* dominated our courts, to be recently challenged by more pragmatic sociologic tendencies. Also, as our universities have developed they have annexed the law schools, and the teachers of the latter are becoming more of scholars and less of mere practitioners. This means a greater recognition of the various philosophies underlying our legal system. And thus, through diverse ways, our teaching and fundamental conceptions of the law are becoming similar in all the Americas.

CHAPTER TWO

Moral Aspects of the Criminal Law

I N PASSING moral judgments as we all sooner or later inevitably do in regard to legal and other human arrangements, we generally oscillate between the appeal to self-evident principles and the appeal to the obvious demands of the specific situation before us. This seems a highly unsatisfactory procedure to those who feel that certainty must be found in one or the other terminus, else all our moral judgments fail for lack of an assured support. This essay is based on the view that such oscillation is under certain logical precautions and scientific systematization the only proper procedure,—that to trust rigid principles regardless of specific consequences makes for inhuman absolutism, while to rely on nothing but the feeling of the moment leads to brutal anarchy. Consider the ethical atomists who think that life breaks itself up into a number of separate autonomous situations, each immediately revealing its own good or proper solution to our conscience, intuition, or intuitive reason, intelligence or common sense. When these moralists are confronted by a challenge to any of their particular judgments, they generally adduce some reason or at least cite an analogous case, thus involving explicitly or implicitly an appeal to some determining principle more abstract and wider than the specific case before them. On the other hand, those who rely on principles to decide specific cases do, and have to, defend these principles by showing that they lead to the proper consequences. By a consideration of some of the ethical problems of the criminal law, I wish to illustrate the truth that the procedure from principles to facts and from facts to principles, without assuming either to be absolute or unquestionable, does not at all lead to complete moral nihilism, but rather clarifies the process of building a systematic view of what

---

The substance of this article was given as a lecture (part of a series on Law and Justice) on the Fenton Foundation and later published in *Yale Law Journal,* Vol. 49, p. 987 (1940). Reprinted by permission of the publisher.

the law should do, even though it tolerates a certain amount of probabilism and pluralism in taking into account the wide variations of social conditions and sentiments.

In the law school's curriculum and in the text-books, the criminal law appears as a distinct and strictly delimited province; and practitioners generally leave it to a separate branch of their profession, by no means the highest in income and prestige. But if you ask the man in the street what he understands by *law* he will generally mention the prohibition against theft, murder or some other punishable offense. As in other cases the layman, while devoid of well-defined and properly elaborated ideas, still touches the root of the matter. The criminal law may properly be viewed not only as a branch but also as a basic phase of the whole legal system.

Jurists often distinguish the criminal from the civil law on the ground that the former is concerned with punishments for violation of those rules of public order to which normal people naturally conform, while the civil law is concerned only with determining the rights of the parties in private transactions. In fact, however, not only does the criminal law today regulate all sorts of private business, but *all* legal provisions (at least in a modern state) have at their back an enforcing machinery that operates through some system of penalties. Consider for instance such requirements as that certain agreements must be in writing or involve a "consideration," that a will must have two or three witnesses, that a valid protest of a note must be within a certain time, or that one may legally charge an interest rate of six per cent. Anyone who ignores these provisions exposes himself to the penalty of losing certain advantages—a loss which may be far more severe than many of the fines for public disorder or for various misdemeanors. A law permitting a man to transfer his property by will is significant only when the beneficiary legatee or devisee can invoke the penal machinery of the state against those who would deprive him of possession. All laws as to property, contract or personal rights may thus be viewed as specifications within the criminal law, specifications as to when the public force will be brought into play to punish nonobedience to its prescriptions.

There are doubtless obvious differences between the extreme penalty of death or life-imprisonment for certain felonies, and the penalties which support the civil law. But it is well to remember that imprisonment for debt has not yet been completely abolished; that the triple damages of the Sherman Anti-Trust Act may deprive you of your home; and when you happen to be put into jail for not obeying an injunction which deprives you of most elementary civil rights, the actual effects on you and your dependents are not much different than if you were punished for committing a crime.

It is sometimes asserted that the civil law protects the private interests of individuals while the criminal law protects the interests of the state or community. But this contrast is of little value. I do not wish to dispute the fact that the interest in preventing sacrilege or other grave public danger was one of the origins of criminal procedure, and that offenses against the king or government have been and still are generally the most severely punished. But it is hardly necessary to call attention to the vital interests of the state not only in protecting but in promoting private industry and commerce from which it derives its support. Surely no interest of the state is so dear to it as the collection of taxes. Yet the non-payment of a real estate tax is not always a crime. An absolute differentiation between the substance of the criminal and of the civil law is indeed clearly impossible so long as the same act may be the basis of either a civil suit or a criminal prosecution. The difference here clearly resolves itself into one of procedure.

In the United States today, it seems very easy to distinguish between criminal and civil procedure on the ground that in the former some state official is in duty bound to prosecute, whereas a civil action is brought by a private individual acting at his pleasure. We must add however that state officials are also bound to bring certain civil suits, and in England the attorney general may intervene in tort cases between private parties. This is not to deny that there are today some differences between civil and criminal procedure, *i.e.*, the one in regard to the burden of proof. But it is well to remember that these differences are far from prevailing in all legal systems and are apt to appear more important in theory than in the actual practice of our jury trials. In any case, up to the second decade of the nineteenth century the common law allowed a private action or "appeal" for murder and other injuries.

These considerations are not intended to deny that legislatures and courts can, do, and should call certain acts criminal and provide some distinctive procedures for dealing with them. The general desire for security demands that everyone know, with a fair degree of certainty, what is and what is not criminal. The fear that some innocent act may be branded as criminal is as horrible as the older paralyzing fear of unconscious unintentional sin. What I wish to insist on is that the criminal law is an integral part of the legal system and is subject to the same considerations which do and should influence the whole. More specifically, the criminal law cannot be distinguished from the rest by any difference of moral principle. Some crimes, to be sure, are shocking; but there are many crimes that are felt to be much less reprehensible than many outrageous forms of injustice, cruelty or fraud, which the law does not punish at all, or else makes their perpetrator liable to money damages in a civil suit. It is well to remember that Moses murdered an Egyptian and fled the country, that Socrates was, by a majority of his fellow citizens that voted, found guilty of a crime, and that George Washington and others would have been treated as criminals if the American Revolution had been as unsuccessful as was the Scotch rebellion under Sir William Wallace. Those who, like Kant, regard obedience to the law as an absolute duty, must logically deny the moral right of any revolution. But this cannot be carried out consistently, since most, if not all, established governments, even the Constitution of the United States, have arisen out of revolutions and military conquest. Some dim, uncomfortable perception of this may be responsible for Kant's remarkable prohibition of any inquiry as to how the existing government acquired its authority.

An adequate discussion of justice in the criminal law must, therefor, deal with all the ethical issues of the law generally, such as the principle of equality, the adjustment of conflicting interests, or the relation between respect for personality and the demands of social responsibility and solidarity. But this study will be limited to a few questions that are in the forefront of current discussion as to the criminal law.

WHAT IS A CRIME?

With this question, we are at once plunged into an ancient and persistent controversy. On one hand, we have the legalists who urge that any act or omission is a crime when, and only when, it is declared to be such by the legislative power or by those who speak with the authority of the law; an act may be sinful, immoral or contrary to the public good, but it is not a crime unless it is legally so declared. On the other hand, we have those who claim this view to be superficial, and who insist that no legislature can or should treat anything as a crime unless it is so in fact or in the nature of things. This issue dates back to the old Greek controversy of the fifth century B.C. between those who saw everything determined by nature and those who pressed the claims of convention or human legislation. To Aristotle may be traced the classical compromise of distinguishing between those acts which are crimes by nature (*mala per se*) and are prohibited among all peoples, and those others (*mala prohibita*) which are prohibited only in certain places by special legislation. This view has been largely influential in molding the classical doctrine of natural rights in the criminal as well as in other branches of the law. In point of fact, however, no one has ever made a critical catalogue of the acts which have actually been prohibited by all peoples at all times. Almost all those who insist that there are *mala per se* put into that class those acts which in an undefined way seem to them to be shocking. But they do not give any clear criterion by which to judge what acts should thus be included and what acts should be excluded from the category of crime.

THE TRADITIONAL MORALISTIC VIEWS OF CRIME

The oldest traditions view crime as a violation of some eternal law set by the gods, nature or reason. These find expression in two forms, the theologic and the rationalist (more properly intuitive). Both have the advantage over the positivist that they do not have to use empirical evidence to establish absolute distinctions between what is and what is not properly a crime.

1. *The theologic point of view.* This is the older and still the most widespread. It regards the criminal law, and indeed all law, as divinely ordained for all time by Manu or by Zeus, given by Jahweh to Moses or to Mohammed by Allah. Without entering into any theologic controversy, it may be granted as an historic fact that communities as a rule do not allow any one who pleases to decide what acts the divine will has ordained as criminal. That is a function left in fact to some recognized authorities, *e.g.*, priests, religiously trained judges, scribes who interpret certain texts, or the like. When the judgment of these authorities can in any way be questioned, there is some attempt to justify it on the basis of reason and human history. Thus great moral-

ists of the Catholic church, such as St. Thomas, are not willing to rest
the distinction between what are and what are not crimes on mere
authority. The divine Will is not despotically arbitrary, but is viewed
as essentially rational and just. Hence in practice, theologic moralists
appeal also to a rationalist view of human nature and experience.

Of course, there are theologians who insist that the essence of crime
is the violation of the divine will, and that our frail human reason cannot determine what is just or unjust for the Perfect Whole. Mankind
is quite accustomed to double standards of morality, different for men
and women, for the state and individual, and for divine and human
persons. Thus it is not wrong for Jahweh to harden Pharaoh's heart
or to send a lying spirit to Ahab in order to punish him. It is not even
wrong to put an evil design into David's heart in order to punish innocent children of Israel by either killing them by the plague or else
depriving them of their parents. But the persistent efforts to explain
such incidents and to justify the ways of God show a general disinclination to view God's law or will as entirely devoid of what seems to us
rational or just.

Moreover, not all sins or violations of God's law are treated by theologians as crimes. Many evil acts are left to the direct punishment of
the divine power here or hereafter, e.g., covetousness, sex relations that
are prohibited by the divine but not by human law, uncharitable attitudes to others, or failure to honor our parents. The Catholic church,
claiming divine authority, does not today urge that the state make it a
penal offense to disbelieve the dogma of trans-substantiation or of the
immaculate conception of the Virgin Mary, or to hold those views as
to the relation of the Holy Ghost to the Father and Son which make
heretics of all the Greek orthodox. If blasphemy is still a crime in some
of our states, it is defended on the alleged ground of protecting the
public peace. Suicide is very often viewed as a direct violation of
divine law. But few care to see criminal punishment meted out to one
who has been unsuccessful in his attempt at it; and we may suspect
that when suicide was treated as a felony, the fact that this deprived
the heirs of the felon of his property and gave it to the king or church
was an important motive or factor in the case.

2. *The point of view of moral intuition.* Of those who have attempted to give us an absolute moral basis for a penal code, Kant is the
foremost. He rejects the claims of all authority, secular or sacred, as

inconsistent with the autonomy of the free will in ethical relations. The universal principle of all moral conduct, the categorical imperative to live so that the maxim of our action can become a principle of universal legislation, is not the source but rather a formula for what conscience, moral faith or "practical reason" immediately dictates as our duty in any specific case. In the end Kant falls back on the assumption that just as our moral conscience tells us that "Thou shalt not kill," is an absolute duty for the individual, so is "You shall kill the murderer" an equally absolute duty for the community. If a society is to be absolved, the last murderer must be executed, else the blood of the victim will be on the heads of those who fail to do so.

While the Kantian theory is fairly close to the popular conscience, which often regards the prevailing *mores* as eternal laws of nature and reason, it fails as a guide in the determination of what specific acts are or ought to be treated as criminal.

Not all violations of moral laws are crimes (*e.g.,* lying). But why is not truth-telling as important for the preservation of the moral order as the protection of property? We all agree that murder should be a crime. But such agreement is purely verbal unless we are agreed as to what is murder. Surely, not all instances of killing can be regarded as criminal, even on Kantian grounds. What distinction does he offer between excusable or even commendable homicide, and murder? No one today regards it as criminal to kill a man in self-defense. But the line between justifiable and unjustifiable fear of attack varies and is somewhat arbitrarily fixed by law. In international relations, it is hopeless to fix a sharp line between an offensive and defensive war, even though in extreme cases the distinction is clear even to those not involved in the combat.

None of us think of the official executioner as a murderer. Though he is obviously not of the highest dignity, and we may not agree with De Maistre that the whole state rests on him, he is still a public servant. Nihilists who condemned and executed some of the brutal underlings of the czar were branded as murderers by his advisers who ordered, one Sunday morning, the shooting of a number of people that came to present a petition. Shall we say that the moral conscience of mankind is clear as to who in these instances was guilty of murder? The soldiers who kill in war are brave heroes, and on both sides they are said to be defending their country. But may not their obedience to their officers make wars of unjust aggression possible?

I am not arguing that there is no such thing as morally revolting criminal murder, simply because in the nature of things there is not any sharp line to define it. That would be like arguing that there is no difference between day and night because there is no sharp line but rather a twilight zone between them. But I am calling attention to the inadequacy of the intuitionists' account which supposes that the common conscience has a clear and universally acknowledged answer as to when an act is or is not criminal.

Similar considerations hold in regard to theft. Apart from existing law, it is hard to say what does and what does not morally belong to another. Especially is this true in modern society when no man can point to anything and say, "This is exclusively the product of my own work in which I received no help from others." For, in fact, the author of a book, or the farmer who raises crops, has been supported by others during his work, and the relative value of his services is largely determined by the conditions created by the legal system. The notion of theft is relatively clear if it denotes taking something in a way that the law prohibits. But on purely moral grounds, apart from the law, it is by no means clear. Is it immoral for a manufacturer to copy the brilliant ideas that his rival has developed? If the design of a dress should be made property by law on the analogy of copyright, then imitating it will become theft. Among many primitive peoples there is no sense of private property in food. But it is a grave theft for one man to sing the personal song of another. Before the copyright laws, there was no conception of property in the literary composition itself. But when the legal rules in regard to property change, our moral duties in respect to it change.

Even if there were an absolute duty to obey the law always (which is dubious), legislation in a modern state would still have to go beyond traditional morality precisely because the latter does not offer sufficiently definite rules to regulate the life of people that in fact have conflicting notions of right and wrong. We see this in the conflicting claims of different classes of society, *e.g.*, employer and employee. The truth is that our specific moral rules are not, as is often assumed, fixed for all time, but vary with changing conditions; and to maintain the order necessary for the good life, we must have the power to terminate controversies definitively. This involves rules that generally are not free from all elements of arbitrariness. Moral duties thus become more definite and clear after the law is enacted. A consideration of the law of marriage and divorce will make this clear. Bigamy is repugnant to the general conscience of today. But was it adulterous for the Old Testament patriarchs to marry more than one wife, even two sisters? Is it adulterous today to marry two sisters successively, if death or divorce comes between the two marriages? Many who regard free love as horrible, see no objection to free divorce. Arbitrary legislation does in fact change our judgments as to what is moral and immoral in given situations, and the law makes crimes of acts that were not so before the legislation took place.

THE POSITIVISTIC VIEW

The positivists who wish to develop a science of criminology, and who believe that a science can deal only with facts of existence, find it difficult to admit that what is a crime is determined by legislation. They are thus forced to maintain that certain acts are criminal by nature, whether committed by men, beasts or even plants. Unfortunately, however, they do not tell us what traits distinguish a criminal from any other act. What for instance makes it criminal for the sensitive plant to feed on insects? Are not birds similarly guilty, and do not fish live by devouring other fish? It seems that the positivists are here following the old doctrine of the Stoic moralists that nature decrees certain acts as impermissible even to animals, so that those who violate this decree are guilty of crimes against nature. But unless we believe in supernatural ordinances or in a devil who interferes with our nature, we must apply the term natural to everything that actually takes place, in the field of legislation as well as in the field of "unnatural" or "abnormal" animal behavior.

The most thoroughgoing attempt to define natural crime is that of Garofalo who identifies it with those harmful actions which shock the moral sense of pity and probity of all civilized people. This moral sense, he holds, is not only unaffected by legislation which makes acts criminal that were not so before, but it is independent also of the circumstances and exigencies of any given epoch.[1] But how can positivists who identify science with determinism hold that social changes can occur without having any effect on what is deemed criminal? Garofalo

---

[1] GAROFALO, CRIMINOLOGY (Tr. Millar 1914) 4.

admits the obvious and well authenticated fact that laws as to what
constitutes crime do vary, but he thinks that the sentiments of pity and
probity are the same among all civilized peoples. But who are civilized
people? The naive answer is: those whose views are like our own,[2]
from which it follows that our ancestors were not, and that other
people with different conceptions of the requisites of pity and probity
are not, civilized. This use of the term *civilized* seems amazingly naive,
but it is supported by the fashionable assumption that there is a cosmic
law according to which all people must, regardless of diverse circumstances in their environment, evolve along the same uniform line of
which we today represent the highest point. There is, however, no
scientific evidence, logical or empirical, for any such law. As a matter
of historic fact, not only do different "civilized" peoples vary in their
moral sense or sentiment as to what pity and probity require, but
within any community there is a large variation in this respect. And
which view, or way of feeling, will prevail depends on temporal
changes that do not follow any one line but are dependent on so
many circumstances or factors that the future is unpredictable.

It is hardly necessary to show that hatred, pugnacity and brutality
have not only been human traits at all times, but have been glorified in
religion and literature. Consider the command in Deuteronomy to exterminate all the inhabitants of a conquered city, or the ferocious ending of the touching psalm "By the Rivers of Babylon," not to mention
the obvious delight in wholesale slaughter in the Book of Esther, or
the record of pious, God-fearing Puritans in their treatment of Indians,
or their participation in the Negro slave traffic.[3] Moreover, when we
reflect on the tortures imposed by the Inquisition, the brutalities of
civil war (and even of the economic struggle), or how certain contemporary rulers have risen to power not only by the practice but by
the very glorification of brutality, it does not seem that the latter trait
is found only among those in prison.

Civilized Italians and Germans at the time that Garofalo wrote
might have been shocked at the suggestion that their people would ever
be capable of perpetrating the cruelties which Fascists and Nazis have

---

[2] *Id.* at 215.

[3] The Boers won a great deal of sympathy when they defended their country
against British imperialism but they had their own record for burning towns,
murdering men and women, and stealing cattle and children. *Letters of David
Livingston* (Aug. 1922) 130 ATLANTIC MONTHLY 212, 213.

exercised on their opponents or even on innocent children who happened to live in Ethiopian villages or to be of Jewish ancestry. Yet those responsible for these acts have become national heroes and their cruelty has become the virtue of fortitude and patriotic devotion to the national state.

Within American society today, there is a violent difference of feeling or sentiment in regard to birth control. There are those who consider it an abominable crime against nature, so that spreading information about it or abetting it should remain a penal offense. On the other hand, there are those who feel strongly that the best interests of society demand that such information be more widely diffused. The question as to which party will prevail cannot be answered by any law of evolution such as Spencer's. It depends upon such factors among others as legislation for improved and more ample housing.

In the end Garofalo admits that besides natural crime there are many offenses which even civilized peoples do and should punish. The latter category will be found to include most of the offenses of our criminal law. Garofalo himself mentions not only political crimes, such as meetings to conspire against the government, seditious utterances, prohibited political demonstrations, refusal to perform required military or other services to the state, irregularities in the conduct of elections, etc., but also clandestine prostitution, smuggling, helping prisoners to escape, and the like. Now if all these are not natural crimes, our prisons contain very many who have not committed any natural crime, while many who practice gross cruelty and improbity in business or elsewhere are not in prison at all. There is therefore no ground for the basic assumption of the "anthropologic" school of criminology, that the physical or mental traits common to prisoners are distinctive of natural criminals.

Positivistic sociologists and jurists as well as moralists often identify crime with acts which are contrary to the social interests or endanger social existence.[4] But the most obvious reflection shows that this begs the question. Acts are criminal not because they *are* harmful, but because they are *deemed* harmful by those who make or interpret the law. The most serious crimes are sometimes those acts that in the judgment of enlightened and heroically unselfish people will best promote the common good, for example, criticism of the errors of established

---

[4] See MERCIER, CRIME AND CRIMINALS (1918).

governments or churches. The history of the martyrs of religion and science amply indicates that acts deemed criminal at a given time in a given community often turn out to be of the greatest value for human life.

In the past the most heinous crimes (judging by the severity of the punishment) have been sacrilege or ceremonial defilement, witchcraft and heresy. Doubtless these were regarded with terror because they were supposed to endanger society by bringing down the wrath of gods that are not careful to discriminate between the guilty and innocent when they send down their lightning or plagues. But what any community regards as most dangerous is not eternally fixed in the nature of things, but varies from time to time and from locality to locality in ways which we cannot always explain. Moreover, it is not always the feeling of danger that makes us regard certain acts as punishable. The causes of social irritation and active resentment are wider. Children in New York have stoned men for wearing straw hats after September 15th, and Mexican peasants have burnt new orange groves planted by foreigners for no other reason than the dislike of any novelty in their vicinity.

THE LEGAL AND THE MORAL

The foregoing discussion has indicated not only the impossibility of identifying the contents of the penal code with eternal morality or with any invariant nature of things, but also the difficulty of regarding legislation as purely arbitrary. Laws must often be changed if our rules of conduct are to facilitate the good life under changing conditions. How this is to be brought about in any given determinate social situation is not something known in advance, but must be determined in the processes of adjustment of our economic and political life. To be effective, the law must have back of it the organized force of the state against those who refuse to conform to it. This force, to be sure, cannot be exercised for any long time unless the law itself is felt by a large part of the community to be in harmony with their prevailing customs and moral views. But we cannot escape legal penalties by trying to show in court that the law is unjust — for example, that the Fugitive Slave Law is inconsistent with the natural rights of man, with the Declaration of Independence, or with judicial dicta to the effect that our constitutional government rests on the principles of freedom and equality. Nor can we escape the penalties of the law of divorce or of military conscription in a Christian country by quoting the words of Christ against divorce or against taking up the sword to kill one's fellow man. Those who are convinced of the existence of injustices in the established law and who struggle for their abolition are more often defeated by general inertia and unreasoning fear of change than by any rational counter argument. Even a convinced and determined majority may for a considerable time be unable to effect the legal change it desires. Hence while the criminal law, like other branches, is largely influenced by various moral views and sentiments, it cannot be identified with the latter — certainly not so long as we admit the possibility of unjust laws, so often used for purposes of oppression.

We hear a good deal of complaint about there being too many statutory crimes. These complaints are rather superficial, if not entirely thoughtless. We need new penal laws in cases where new conditions cannot be adequately dealt with by reliance on customary ways. This is obviously the case where, having introduced, e.g., the secret ballot, we need to protect its secrecy, or having introduced telephony, we need to protect the privacy of communications. Thus also, when modern methods of canning goods are introduced, the community of consumers needs better protection than the old laws or ways of doing business afford. Of course, legislative enactments as to crime may soon become obsolescent. But that is not an inherent evil if legislatures are as quick to repeal old laws as to enact new ones.

It is of the utmost importance that the law be just. But it is also important that our conception of justice and the nature of things be not so rigid as to prevent experiments in legislation to attain optimum conditions. For since we lack omniscience as to all the possible forms of social adjustment, experimentation, or the process of learning from experience, is indispensable. Law and morality can coincide only in the fundamental assumptions as to the proper procedure to enable us to correct our mistakes. Their common ideal is thus like that of science, to wit, a system that corrects itself by the process of testing principles by their consequences, and conversely, judging actual consequences in the light of principles.

Judges and jurists are tempted to take the position that they have to deal only with the existing law and need not be concerned with what the law should be. And this is, because of the principle of strict interpretation, easier to maintain in the criminal than in any other branch of the law. Nevertheless, in the end it is impossible for any thoughtful and sensitive person dealing with the criminal law consistently to refrain from passing moral judgment. And such judgment exerts a powerful influence on the actual administration of the civil law. Yet, the legislative question of what acts should be made criminal and which should no longer be so treated cannot be settled by ethical principles alone. To apply the latter we need to have factual knowledge as to what are going to be the various consequences of the enactment or repeal to the different individuals that will be affected thereby. As the complexity and uncertainty of future social events generally make it next to impossible to obtain complete knowledge on this point, and as even the acquisition of some approximate knowledge open to our various social sciences involves enormous difficulties, moralists have tended to ignore this factual side altogether and have asserted that right is right regardless of all consequences. This has found expression in the maxim *fiat justitia pereat mundus,* or *fiat justitia ruat coelum.*

It is easy enough to dismiss this as a lazy evasion or even as inherently absurd. It is more difficult to determine the amount of truth back of it which has made this assertion appeal to so many noble spirits. We can begin the latter task if we realize the inadequacy of the maxim that the good or ill of any act is to be judged by its consequences only. For this does not determine which consequences are to be deemed good and which are to be regarded as bad. And any discriminating test which applies to consequences should be applicable as well to the original act. If nothing has any inherent or intrinsic goodness in itself, neither can the consequences have it. The insistence on taking the consequences of an act into consideration is valid only if we realize that the problem is one of balancing immediate or present goods or ills against future ones. This is not a solution of the problem of ethical evaluation, but it calls our attention to our fundamental difficulty, which is that of determining the relative weights of the different interests that are often in conflict. The principle of the greatest good to the greatest number not only fails to give us a common denominator or common unit for the different kinds of value, but it is not possible to take all men and women equally into account. The obligation to those of our own family or community, state or nation, generally seems to outweigh the interests of any equal number of others, and it does not seem that our obligation to remotely future generations is as great as to more immediate ones. In the absence of any accurate determination of the relative weights of different obligations, all sorts of variations of opinion in this respect are possible.

When we consider any course of harmful conduct, our first impulse is to urge the enactment of a law to prohibit it; but on reflection we become aware of the enormous cost of bringing the criminal law into play. This includes not only the direct cost of policing and detection of crime, of judicial procedure and penal institutions, but also the indirect costs of social fear, spying, and the often unsavory effects of criminal proceedings, as for example, in the case of adultery.

JUSTICE IN PUNISHMENT

When we raise the question of punishment, we are met at the outset with the challenge, what right has the state to punish at all? This challenge sometimes comes from determinists who hold that the criminal could not help doing what he did, and sometimes it comes from those who maintain that society itself, through the conditions and institutions which it tolerates, is ultimately the cause and therefore responsible for the offensive acts.

Though it is customary for writers on ethics or penology to discuss in this connection the question of determinism versus free will, that is really not necessary for our purpose. When we are considering whether we should or should not punish certain individuals, it is irrelevant to argue that no one can help doing what he does. For against such an argument it is fair to reply as the irate father did to the wayward son who used it: "If no one can help doing what he does, then I can't help punishing you." The truth is that the ethical question is not the metaphysical one, whether the human will as such is or is not absolutely uncaused, but rather how to discriminate properly between those who should and those who should not be held accountable for legally prohibited acts. And here the prevailing ethical conscience today seems to recognize a common sense distinction between voluntary and involuntary acts, and generally holds that no one should be punished for any act in which his will did not enter.

I shall try to show later that this principle is subject to some important qualifications. But if we accept it, as in the main we must, we have to answer those who claim that criminals are a special class whose acts are not normally voluntary because they are determined by special physical, biologic or mental conditions.

IS THERE A SPECIAL PHYSICAL CAUSE OF CRIME?

Crime and punishment were, up to the middle of the nineteenth century, objects for the consideration of moralists, philanthropic reformers and prison officials. It is to the credit of Lombroso and his associates that they conceived that the matter should interest scientists, that since the criminal is a human being, reliable knowledge of the nature of crime should be the aim of the science of anthropology.

As the most advanced science of their day was physics, they naively assumed that the science of criminality could be established firmly by viewing crime as a purely physical phenomenon having physical causes. On this assumption they proceeded to measure the physical traits of criminals in prison and found all sorts of stigmata, such as epilepsy, anesthesia and the like, which they attributed to degeneracy or atavism. This movement acquired great prestige, not only because it brought in the fashionable ideas of popular science, but also because it appealed to certain humane feelings. By insisting that the criminal is not a normal human being who freely chooses to break the law, but is one who suffers from certain defects, inherited or inherent in his physical constitution, they sought to show the futile cruelty of the usual forms of punishment and the necessity of treating the criminal with the same absence of resentment with which enlightened communities now treat the sick and the insane.

The great weakness of this school is its altogether inadequate conception of what constitutes scientific procedure or scientific proof.

In their haste to be scientific, the members of this school did not at the outset stop to ask precisely what was the phenomenon which they wanted to study and explain. For obviously if crime is a violation of the law, few of us go through life without committing some crime such as the violations of traffic rules or rules as to income tax returns, declaration of goods bought abroad, etc. It would be a most illuminating study to determine why so many of us do fail to obey laws that we thoroughly approve. We should not expect a simple answer when there are so many different factors which divert people from the path which they recognize as honest or reasonable. The problems of health are relatively simple since they depend on more verifiable physical factors. Yet who would expect a simple answer to the question, why are not people perfectly healthy, or what causes disease? There are many different kinds of disease, and of only a few do we have an adequate idea as to their causes. How naive is it then to ask for the cause of the much more complex phenomena of crime, which are influenced not only by physical and biologic factors but also by training, association and personal elements, which are seldom if ever available for examination. In point of fact, the positivists do not study the causes of crime in this wider sense. What they really study are the traits of prisoners, among whom are some who have been wrongfully convicted and have not actually violated any law. Nor are all who have committed crimes to be found in prison, not even all who have been apprehended and found guilty. For some have been fined or have had sentence suspended.

Do these prisoners form a physically homogeneous group? Some are there for purely political offenses, some for non-payment of certain debts, others because of embezzlement or fraudulent stock transactions, and some for crimes of passion. Even a single category such as theft represents most diverse types of people and motives.

Now if the analogies of biologic science are to guide us, we should not expect the measurement of the outer physical features of all these men and women to give us the cause of crime. At best it may reveal some fact or element of the situation, certainly not anything like a sufficient cause.

Now not only have the actual measurements been hasty and inaccurate, but these lovers of scientific procedure fail to observe the most elementary caution of statistical inquiry, namely, to check their generalizations by inquiring first whether the same stigmata which they find in prison do not exist outside of prison among people of the same situation in life. Then, too, even if it were true that certain stigmata are more prevalent in prison than among the same class of people outside, it does not necessarily follow that these stigmata are, or indicate, the cause of crime. Not all correlations have direct causal significance. The stigmata may be the effects of the kind of life that the prisoners have lived and perhaps even the effect of the prison itself. There are people who claim to be able to recognize with a fair degree of accuracy criminals of a certain kind. There is little experimental evidence for this claim; but even if it were demonstrated, it would not follow that there are hereditary causes for crime. All groups seem to develop noticeable characters, so that some can recognize sailors, clergymen, actors and other occupational groups that are not at all hereditary and hardly attributable to any definite physical cause.

These methodologic observations do not deny that there may be physical factors in crime, but they do warn us against accepting at its face value the mass of "evidence" gathered by the positivistic school. On the whole, when we consided how artificial is the distinction between the criminal and the non-criminal, we need not be surprised to find criminologists who assert that there is little physical difference between the two.[5]

There are doubtless sick and insane men and women among those condemned for crime; and it may be that these unfortunates are more easily seduced or led into crime than those who can take better care of themselves. They should receive treatment in hospitals or insane asylums. But there is no reason for ignoring distinctions between crime on the one hand and disease or insanity on the other. If the criminal be viewed as one who has failed to adjust himself to a social environment, which of us is properly adjusted? Certainly not the persecuted saints or prophets.

If statistical studies show that certain crimes are more frequent in the summer than in the winter months, it does not follow that this indicates a direct relation between heat and criminality. There are seasonal variations of employment which may play a more direct role here. There is also the social factor of the opportunity for certain crimes, when more people are out in the streets or in certain thoroughfares, gatherings, etc. This may be a much closer explanation of the variations of criminality in our northern and southern states.

ARE CRIMINALS FEEBLE-MINDED?

In view of the difficulty of measuring the intelligence of criminals who are not caught and put in prison, it is not easy to establish their relative intelligence. Every knave may be a fool, but there is no reason to believe that foolishness is restricted to those who break the criminal law. It is well to insist that those sent to prison have failed in their plans. If then we take those who have failed in any business, might we not find them of a lower mental average than the rest of the population? Of course, those who fail in the business of crime are very often those who have been exploited. Feeble-minded women especially

---

[5] Lombroso, L'Homme Criminel (1895) 324 claims that prisoners lack sensitiveness. This is flatly denied by Joly in Le Crime 113. See Sutherland, Principles of Criminology (1934) c. 5.

are no match for those captains of crime who sit behind the lines and do not suffer from the casualties of the social war. No one can deny that the rich with a staff of able lawyers can find their way through and around the law; and there is no reason to suppose that the "fences" who buy up jewelry from thieves have a lower I.Q. than the average of the communities where they live.

IS CRIME AN INSTANCE OF ATAVISM?

The theory of evolution has brought into vogue the attempt to explain all puzzling social phenomena as survivals of the past or as instances of reversion to the state of our remote ancestors. In line with this we have the theory of crime as an atavistic relapse into the primitive or savage state. But what basis is there for identifying crime with the state of savages? Most of the savages known to us obey their customary rules with perhaps greater regularity than we do, and there is no reason to suppose that our remote ancestors exceeded us in the number of perjuries, forgeries, embezzlements, fraudulent bankruptcies, counterfeiting, smuggling, safe-cracking and the like. Even the art of pick-pocketing can hardly be regarded as a reversion to an earlier state of mankind.

To this Lombroso replies that the tendency to these crimes existed in germ in our savage ancestors. But if, according to the theory of evolution, all civilization is a maturation of the germs latent in savage society, atavism can hardly be distinctive of crime. More important, however, is it to note that while we use the word savagery as synonymous with cruelty, it is not true that savages (*e.g.*, those in the South Sea Islands) are always more cruel than civilized peoples. The popular impression to that effect is due to the fact that we are less likely to notice those forms of cruelty to which we have become accustomed. It is not necessary to overlook or minimize the vices of primitive people. But it is well to note that they become demoralized when first brought into contact with more powerful, civilized people. This is due not only to the exploitation by these civilized invaders, but also to the fact that demoralization naturally follows whenever any people's habits and customs are rapidly changing.

Similar to the foregoing is the theory that crime represents that feral strain in mankind that cannot adjust itself to the processes of civilization. History shows that many peaceful people become criminals under specific social conditions, *e.g.*, the sturdy beggars in Tudor England when people were deprived of the support they used to receive from the monasteries, or when their farms were turned by their lords into pasture land. How many descendants of law-abiding families became brigands (Klephtai) when Greece was subjugated by Turkey, or when the conditions of border life in America put a premium on the life of the ruffian or the land swindler?

CRIME AND NATURAL SELECTION

The uncritical haste to apply the theory of natural selection to the phenomena of crime leads, as in other cases, to a confusion between moral and biological categories. It is fortunately not necessary for our present purpose to point out the limitations of the category of natural selection in biology itself. That is at best a name for a large number of factors, many of which are unknown. It is sufficient to insist that biologic fitness to survive means a greater birth-rate than a death-rate and that there is no reason to assume that saints multiply more rapidly than sinners, or that moral heroes and martyrs are those who preserve their lives longest. The distinction between the moral and the biologic is also confused by regarding gregariousness or sociability as an unmitigated virtue.[6]

The late Professor Giddings and his disciple Hall maintained that on the whole the process of converting immoralities into positive crimes is one of the most powerful means by which society in the long run eliminates the socially unfit and gives an advantage in the struggle for existence to the thoughtful, the considerate, the far-seeing and the compassionate, so lifting its members to higher planes of instinct and character. While such a consummation would be highly desirable, neither Giddings nor Hall has given us any adequate evidence that that is actually the case, certainly not enough to shake the contrary conviction that the criminal law has often been an instrument of

---

[6] Some years ago the benevolent anarchist Prince Kropotkin published a book, MUTUAL AID AS A FACTOR IN EVOLUTION (1902), which appealed to certain moralists, though not at all to biologists. Although many instances of mutual aid among animals were there adduced, there is no evidence that it is a factor in evolution, and no organic developments are traced to it. Certainly, non-gregarious animals, like the tiger or the snake, manage to survive. Indeed, the extremely individualistic uni-cellular organisms seem to have survived for longer periods than any others. Nor is mutual helpfulness really an absolute moral good. The mutual aid of brigands or gangs of political corruptionists makes them all the more dangerous to society; and the unquestioning subordination of individuals to the state threatens today to destroy all the values of civilization.

oppression by which the ruling powers have manage to keep people in subjection. It is true that in all countries at all times the most serious crime is that which endangers not the community as a whole but the particular rulers. Thus, in Russia, both under the czar and under the present government, ordinary murder is punishable by a limited term in prison, but any attempt to change the form of government is a capital offense. This does not come under the exception which Giddings admits, namely the mistaken zeal which sometimes brands harmless acts as crimes. It is rather a felt necessity, on the part of all governing classes. And when it prevents, as it often does, any agitation for any change in government, religious views, or moral code, it becomes a hindrance to real progress.

Theories which regard crime as a social maladjustment can recognize that since social conditions change, an individual who is not adapted to one set of social conditions might well be adapted to another set, so that the cure for crime might be effected by eliminating certain social arrangements rather than human beings. And those who argue that the progress of civilization consists in raising our standards of conduct, even though that means increasing the number of criminals, are blandly begging the question. What is the good of such progress purchased at the cost of preventable misery and degradation?

In general, the contention that those who manage to adjust themselves to the existing legal system are the abler ones, rests upon an ambiguity between a tautology and an absurdity. It is a tautology, of course, that those who are able to adjust themselves are thus able. It is an absurdity that those who are able to adjust themselves to the existing law are necessarily superior morally. Under different (and perhaps better) conditions, the others might shine much more. Unless, therefore, we assume that the existing law is identical with the absolute and unchanging moral order, we cannot maintain that those who are not adjusted are necessarily morally inferior to those who succeed. For among the former have been political and religious martyrs, men like John Huss, Jerome of Prague (who blessed those who burnt him), Thomas More, and the like; while among those who have succeeded within the law have been all sorts of tyrants and ruthless exploiters. There are doubtless many who drift into crime and then into prison because of moral weakness or defect. But this does not deny that in the effort to keep out of prison, poverty is a serious handicap. So long as the law of property makes its distribution unequal, it cannot be said that everyone at birth has an equal chance, and that those who succeed in being economically comfortable are therefore proved thereby to be morally superior.

THE ECONOMIC CAUSE OF CRIME

We come now to the argument that the cause of crime, or at least the main cause, is to be found in economic conditions; and since society is responsible for these economic conditions, society itself is responsible for the crime. On this view it is as profoundly foolish to devote our attention to the punishment of the criminal as to concentrate on the swatting of mosquitoes while we allow the breeding ground to continue.

This argument raises two questions. First, are economic conditions the sole cause of crime; and second, if so, can we dispense with punishment?

That crime has its sole cause in a given economic system is a proposition which has been fanatically maintained and fanatically denied. But if we abandon the monistic prejudice of trying to explain everything as due to one cause, the question is not a difficult one. Crime is certainly not unrelated to economic conditions, but there is no simple ratio between crime and poverty. There are many crimes of passion which affect the prosperous as well as the needy. But it must be admitted that men of wealth have a greater opportunity of escaping imprisonment. They have more means for securing witnesses and documents, hiring more skillful lawyers, etc.[7] It has been argued that a relatively small number of prisoners have committed crimes because of actual lack of food. But who supposes that economic need ends where the line of actual starvation is passed? Moreover, it is a fact that men and women are demoralized by extreme poverty to the extent that they cannot bring up their children properly. Morrison mentions in this connection that the number of female beggars is less than the number of male beggars though the former are more often in need. But the obvious answer to this is that successful mendicancy requires a certain energy, and that women not only cling more to ideas of respectability but when they go in for mendicancy, many of them soon drift into prostitution. Many writers have urged that mendicancy cannot be due

---

[7] ETTINGER, THE PROBLEM OF CRIME (1932) 149.

to extreme poverty, because there have been instances of able bodied beggars who are offered opportunities to work at fair remuneration.[8] This argument seems to me to show a singular lack of social imagination. In the first place, it ignores the fact that none of us find it easy to change our occupation, even though originally we may have made great efforts to avoid it. How many of those engaged in the kind of soliciting that is regarded as respectable, *e.g.,* for subscriptions to periodicals or to new stock companies, would change their occupation if offered the kind of work and pay which Monot and the others offered? We must also remember that the granting of alms was regarded as a virtue long before begging for alms (when not done by organized groups) became a crime.

But while there is no simple proportionality between economic distress and criminality, the causal relation between the two cannot be ignored. The inmates of our jails and prisons are, in overwhelming proportions, poor people. Of course, we must take into account that the poor are also in the great majority outside of prison. But even allowing for this, the wealthy certainly have the advantage of attaining their ends by legal ways which are not open to the poor. In the business world, it is common for certain powerful financial interests to demand that they be allowed a liberal share in certain profitable undertakings, for their ill will is very dangerous. This was notoriously the case a few years ago in the tobacco trade. Railroads also have been compelled to engage in certain deals in order to give controlling bankers an opportunity to make commissions on the flotation of certain loans. In the same way, politically powerful individuals extort money from business men by compelling them to contribute to party funds which they control. But the man without wealth or political power has no such lever. He has to use the threat of physical force or blackmail. This does not deny the great evil of the latter. But though the poor are more numerous and more needy, they are not inherently more criminal or even more ruthless in attaining their ends.

We may conclude then that economic conditions are a very important cause of crime. But it is obvious that not every one in a given economic situation will be equally tempted or will as readily yield to temptation. Psychic dispositions and previous habits and associations

---

[8] MORRISON, CRIME AND ITS CAUSES (1891) 105; LEROY-BEAULIEU, L'ETAT MODERNE (1900) 30.

enter into the situation. On the whole it can safely be asserted that the greatest resistance to criminal temptation is steady employment. If, then, a crime curve be plotted along the line of income, we shall not find the former straight. We shall, I think, find the maximum in the classes that have the lowest income, with a lower rate for peasants who continue to live on their family lands even if on a rather low income level. There seems to be an increase in criminality when boys and girls try to improve their lot by going to the cities where the opportunity for crime is greater and settled custom exerts less force. The influence, however, of past tradition may last for a considerable time. Thus, the smaller criminality among the foreign born is to be explained not only by their age distribution but by the persistence of their old home training, while the increased criminality of their more Americanized children is due to the fact that those accustomed to the old world discipline have difficulty in transmitting it to their children who are living under new conditions.

Does the existence of economic causes remove the necessity of punishment? The fact that some conditions leading to crime are removable does not prove that all are so. But what is even more important is to be on guard against the assumption that the elimination of social conditions can be effected at once. If, as human experience indicates, this is not so easy, we may well ask of our reformers: what do you propose to do with those guilty of rape, incendiary murder or the like? Abolish the cause? Admirable, when feasible. But so long as these offenses do occur, do you propose to do nothing to the offender? Even if you propose to reform him, must you not detain him against his will? And is not such detention a punishment?

While these counter questions are legitimate, they do not go sufficiently to the root of the matter. For back of all the arguments against the right or duty of punishment is the natural and just, if inadequately formulated, resentment against the stupid and ineffective cruelty of our whole penal system. It was the conservative President Taft, later Chief Justice of the Supreme Court, who characterized our criminal law as a disgrace to civilization.

THE PRINCIPLE OF INDIVIDUAL RESPONSIBILITY
FOR VOLUNTARY ACTS

The main principle of just criminal punishment, one that is generally regarded as self-evident, is that one shall never be answerable for the crime of anyone else, and for his own only to the extent that it is voluntary. Before the advent of the Nazi regime in Germany, it would have been easier to argue that these principles have been established as the result of the long process of human evolution. But recent experience, if not critical reflection, should make us hesitate to ignore the past experience of the human race which has by no means always accepted the principle of no punishment except for individual voluntary action. The whole of human history testifies to the fact that individuals are punished for the acts of those related to them. Few readers of the Bible, I imagine, have felt outraged at the fact that when Achan sins, his innocent children are also killed. And today, when the head of a family is put in prison, fined or killed, the members of his family are in fact punished, though in not quite the same way. Furthermore, as a result of the first World War, Germany was made to pay reparations, and the burden fell upon the innocent children who had no part and could in no way prevent the invasion of Belgium and the destruction which it involved. Was this unjust? By no means, if we recognize collective responsibility. It is obvious that in many relations the family or the nation rather than the individual is regarded as the moral unit. This does not deny the individual's responsibility for his own acts. But what acts are his own alone? It is not always possible to reduce social action to that of a number of independent atomic units each responsible for his own deeds, since in fact we are parts of each other's fate; and punishment or reward of any one individual naturally affects others. Thus the members of a family or of a nation who acquire a certain estate must necessarily participate in the liabilities of that estate. Bills of attainder seemed quite just when estates were given to the head of a family and were forfeited when he proved disloyal. It is only in recent times when the economic unity of the family is no longer so strong that such acts have been looked upon as unjust. So long as we profit from the virtues of other members of our family (or nation) we must be prepared to pay the penalty of their faults.

Just as the history of religious literature impresses one with the fact that the most dangerous sins have been involuntary ones, so does the history of the criminal law reveal the fact that unintentional acts have been and to some extent still are punished. Even in Biblical law the man who unintentionally caused the death of another was subject to the same penalties as if he had done it intentionally. The Deuterono-

mic reform consisted in providing a city of refuge for the one who was
the innocent cause of death; but he could be killed with impunity if
caught outside of its gate. In general the conditions of modern life
and the emphasis on the subjective elements in our thought, have
stressed the voluntary phase of conduct in the criminal law as elsewhere. We no longer punish animals or inanimate objects for injuries
that result from them. The law no longer holds me responsible when
I am deprived of the usual freedom of action by purely external physical forces, *e.g.,* when I am pushed or thrown. Similarly, I am not a
free agent in the legal sense if purely physiologic factors prevent normally conscious action, *e.g.,* if I faint and fall or if my arm gets para-
lyzed and I cannot do the things that the law requires me to do. In
more recent times the law is beginning to give more recognition to
psychic hindrances to normally voluntary action. It is now considered
useless cruelty to punish those who are so insane that they do not know
what they are doing, or cannot distinguish between right and wrong.
The deterrent value of such punishment would be almost nil. I say
almost, for it may be argued that the deterrent effect of punishment
depends upon the certainty of its being applied, and that this is somewhat diminished when there is the ability to hire experts to convince
a jury that the one who committed a criminal act was not sane at the
time he did it.

Whether because psychiatry is not yet an exact science, or whether
because there are so many intermediate cases between the completely
(if only momentarily) insane and those who are perfectly in control of
their thoughts and acts (if indeed there be any such), any sharp line
of division between the legally responsible and those not so responsible
is necessarily somewhat arbitrary. The whole criminal law would certainly break down if any one could escape the legal penalty because of
ignorance or confusion as to what is right and what is wrong. If yield-
ing to the desire to take attractive articles without pay should cease
to be theft when called kleptomania, then the law against stealing
might as well be abolished. Alienists and others who have not been
trained to rigorous critical standards of scientific evidence or proof are
apt to be misled by highly developed technical terminologies into
overestimating the amount of determinate and verifiable knowledge
at their disposal. This shows itself in the readiness with which different
experts testify on opposite sides of a case. Under the circumstances it

is natural for judges, who see too many criminals escape the just penalties of the law, to look with distrust at any extension of this opportunity under the guise of science. Possibly some judges are unduly conservative. But it is not necessary for our purpose to decide the exact extent to which psychiatry can at present tell us whether a man has acted under such abnormal compulsion as not to know what he was doing or not be able to distinguish between right and wrong. It is sufficient for us to realize that relatively few of us are so free from all inner compulsions as to realize perfectly what we are doing, or to know adequately the difference between right and wrong. The prevalence of human error, regret and disappointment seems to indicate that most of us are in the intermediate zone, and if there is to be any legal responsibility at all, it must include many doubtful cases.

There are also various reasons why certain people may by rule be exempted from the normal workings of the criminal law. It is not feasible to give ordinary officials the right to arrest or prosecute the ambassador of a foreign country, or the king or other head of our own state. If these do commit forbidden acts, our remedy must be sought elsewhere than in the ordinary criminal law. Children below a certain age cannot be tried at all because of the presumption that they do not know what they are doing. But like all conclusive presumptions, this one contains an element of fiction. The act of a child between six and seven, for instance, may actually be more intelligently and consciously planned than the acts of many a low-witted adult. But on the whole, the amount of injury done by children under seven that could possibly be minimized by prosecuting them (and going through the difficult task of determining whether they knew what they were doing), does not warrant doing violence to the general sense of the sacredness of childhood. And so we draw an arbitrary line at the age of seven or so.

THE RETRIBUTIVE, EXPIATORY OR RETALIATORY THEORY

Against the doubt as to whether the state has any right to punish at all, this theory maintains it to be a positive moral duty. It regards crime as a violation or disturbance of the divine or moral order. When Cain kills Abel, the very earth cries for vengeance. The moral order can be restored, or the violation atoned for only by inflicting evil (generally pain) upon the guilty one.

It is easy, far too easy, to dismiss this theory with the remark that it is a remnant of the barbaric conception of vengeance as an absolute duty. The sentiment of just vengeance or retribution is too deeply grounded in human nature, and embodied in too many moral and religious codes, to be thus lightly dismissed. It is profoundly foolish to suppose that anyone can by the free use of ugly epithets, eradicate the desire to return a blow or to give active expression to the resentment against injury. It is not only barbaric people who regard punishment as a duty. We have already noted that the highly idealistic or spiritual book of Deuteronomy deemed that one had a right to avenge the killing of a kinsman even when the killing was accidental. And the stern Greek moralist, Aeschylus, would not deny altogether the duty of a son to avenge the murder of his father even against his mother. The traditional code of honor still prevailing in Europe is that a gentleman must, at the risk of his life, resent an insult to the extent of seeking to remove it with the blood of the offender. In the clubs of European gentlemen, the English and Americans used to be looked down upon, because they would not fight duels. But even with us, popular sentiment was expressed by Theodore Roosevelt who regarded a man as a poltroon who, when his wife was insulted, called on a policeman instead of exercising a gentleman's duty to knock the offender down. And this view seems to prevail among those nations that are generally regarded as most enlightened. To defend the national honor one must fight or make reprisals for insults. In religion, this sentiment expresses itself in the orthodox theory that heaven would be less fair or that God's justice would be tarnished if there were no hell for the sinners, even when the sins are not the result of free will. Kant, who went to extremes in putting duty for duty's sake foremost, expressed an undoubtedly wide sentiment when he urged that we could not regard a world as moral if in it virtue went unrewarded or sin unpunished.

But does this retributive theory offer us a criterion whereby to discriminate between just and unjust punishment? Kant offers us the *jus talionis,* the principle of equality between the crime and the penalty. This sounds simple in the case of murder, a life for a life. But it is obviously not capable of being extended. Crime and punishment are different things. Can they really be equated? What penalty equals the crime of forgery, perjury or kidnapping? For the state to exercise the same amount of fraud or brutality on the criminal that the criminal exercised on his victim would be demoralizing to any community. In point of fact, not even the rigoristic Kant has the courage of his hard convictions; and he refuses to prescribe the death penalty in such cases as dueling and infanticide or to all those engaged in a rebellion. Indeed, he hesitates at prescribing a death penalty in cases where such penalty will not act as a deterrent.   Moreover, if we accept the *jus talionis* as absolute, we make it immoral to pardon a criminal. Yet, the moral and religious conscience of mankind has always regarded charity or mercy as of supreme value and forgiveness has been preached as a divine virtue.

But if the old form of the *lex talionis,* an eye for an eye or a tooth for a tooth, sounds too barbaric today, may we not reformulate the retributive theory and put it thus: Everyone is to be punished alike in proportion to the gravity of his offense or to the extent to which he has made others suffer? As Mittermeier, the leading criminalist of the early nineteenth century once put it, "The penalty which transgresses by even one atom the seriousness of the crime is unjust." But by what yardstick or measure can we determine the precise degree of offensiveness, or the exact amount of suffering that the criminal has imposed on the victim or on all those who depend on the latter? And how can we measure the severity of the punishment? Historically the plea for equality has meant a reaction or revulsion against the ignoring of it in previous criminal laws: let us have no more favorites, no more tariff of offenses with different rates according to the social standing of the offenders as in Anglo-Saxon England or in the France of the ancient regime. But what is the same punishment? Is the same fine, for example, productive of the same effect on rich and poor? Or does the same number of years in prison have the same effect on different individuals regardless of their diverse temperaments or physique? If we took the principle of equality literally as absolute, we should not have any right to make any distinction in the punishment of a first offender and a hardened criminal, between a man acting under natural passion, for example an outraged father or husband, and a shrewdly calculating villain.

Despite the foregoing and other limitations of the retributive theory, it contains an element of truth which only sentimental foolishness can ignore. The sentiment that injuries should be avenged still prevails in the relations between nations and cannot be ignored within the life of any community. The problem of enlightened social morality is not to suppress the natural desires of human beings. Such suppression may itself be vain or cruel. Morality should aim to eliminate or minimize the brutality of natural vengeance or such results as would breed more general evil than the suffering of any particular injury.

If the natural desire for vengeance is not met and satisfied by the orderly procedure of the criminal law we shall revert to the more bloody private vengeance of the feud and of the vendetta. We must remember that lynch law is not a recent American invention but rather the primitive form of public justice, and that the formal procedure of the criminal law is only a more rational expression of this primitive demand. The criminal law deals not with a kingdom of heaven but with actual men and women of flesh and blood living on earth.

While the principle of equality cannot be literally carried out it does suggest that no system of punishments will be considered just if it shows evidence of what is generally considered favoritism.

THE REFORM THEORY

The most popular theory today is that the proper aim of criminal procedure is to reform the criminal so that he may become adjusted to the social order. A mixture of sentimental and utilitarian motives gives this view its great vogue. With the spread of humane feeling and the waning of faith in the old conception of the necessity for inflicting pain in the treatment of children and those suffering from mental disease, there has come a revulsion at the hard-heartedness of the old retributive theory. The growing belief in education and in the healing powers of medicine encourages people to suppose that the delinquent may be re-educated to become a useful member of society. Even from the strictest economic point of view, individual men and women are the most valuable assets of any society. Is it not better to save them for a life of usefulness rather than punish them by imprisonment, which generally makes them worse after they leave than before they entered?

There are, however, a number of highly questionable assumptions back of this theory which need to be critically examined.

We have already had occasion to question the assumption that crime is a physical or mental disease. We may now raise the question whether it is curable and if so at what cost to society? Benevolent social reformers are apt to ignore the amount of cold calculating business shrewdness among criminals. Some hot-blooded ones may respond to emotional appeal; but they are also likely to backslide when opportunity or temptation comes along. Human beings are not putty that can be remolded at will by benevolent intentions. The overwhelming majority of our criminals have been exposed to the influence of our school system which we have at great cost tried to make as efficient as possible. Most criminals are also religious, as prison chaplains can testify. Yet with all our efforts school education and religion do not eliminate crime. It has not even been demonstrated that they are progressively minimizing it. Nor does the record of our special reformatories for young offenders prove that it is always possible to reform even young people so that they will stay reformed for any length of time. The analogy of the criminal law to medicine breaks down. The surgeon can determine with a fair degree of accuracy when there is an inflamed appendix or cancerous growth, so that by cutting it out he can remove a definite cause of distress. Is there in the complex of our social system any one cause of crime which any social physician can as readily remove on the basis of similarly verifiable knowledge?

Let us abandon the light-hearted pretention that any of us knows how all cases of criminality can be readily cured, and ask the more modest and serious question: to what extent *can* criminals be reeducated or re-conditioned so that they can live useful lives? It would indeed be illiberal dogmatism to deny all possibility and desirability of effort along this line. Yet we must keep in mind our human limitations.

If the causes of crime are determined by the life of certain groups, it is foolish to deal with the individual as if he were a self-sufficient and self-determining system. We must deal with the whole group to which he naturally belongs or gravitates and which determines his morale. Otherwise we have to adapt him completely to some other group or social condition, which is indeed a very difficult problem in social engineering.

And here we must not neglect the question of cost. When we refer to any measure as impracticable we generally mean that the cost is too great. There is doubtless a tremendous expense in maintaining our present system of punishment. But this expense is not unlimited. Suppose that fiendish perpetrators of horrible crimes on children could be reformed by being sent first for several years to a special hospital. Will people vote large funds for such purposes when honest law-abiding citizens so often cannot get adequate hospital facilities? Suppose that we find that a certain social environment or that an elaborate college course will reform a burglar or gunman, would our community stand for the expense when so many worthy young people cannot afford to go to college because they have to go to work? We certainly should not give even the appearance of reward for criminality. Let us not forget that there is always a natural resentment in any society against those who have attacked it. Will people be satisfied to see one who is guilty of horrible crimes simply reformed, and not give vent to the social horror and resentment against the miscreant? It is difficult to believe that any such course would not result in a return to personal vengeance on the part of the relatives or friends of the victim.

A crucial instance of the inadequacy of the reform theory is the case of a man who we are fairly certain will not commit the given offense again. A burglar, for instance, in trying to enter a house breaks his leg so that he can never again engage in that enterprise. A man in desperation kills one who has ruined his family life and it becomes obvious that he will never again have a chance to be in a similar situation. Or take the case of one who can for any reason convince us that the criminal act itself has sobered him so that never again will he commit such an act. What more can reform achieve in these cases? Shall we then close the account and let the guilty one off? That not only would arouse general resentment but would open the gates to all sorts of abuses and would certainly so encourage crime that the suffering of innocent people would increase.

It has been argued that on the theory of protection to society there should be no punishment for one who is no longer capable of doing harm. But this ignores the fact that the law contemplates not only the individual at the bar but all others who might be tempted to commit similar offenses even under conditions not quite the same.

PUNISHMENT AS A MEANS OF PREVENTING CRIME

If we look at the criminal as one who assails or endangers the proper life of the community, it is not only our right but our duty to defend, if not ourselves, at least our dependents. Primitive communities effect this by getting rid of the unruly member through death or outlawry. In the course of time, this is largely replaced by fine or imprisonment. Societies, however, never abandon the effort to minimize crime by punishing the offenders. We do this by incapacitating the criminal either through death or detention, and by deterring him and others through the example of the painful consequences of crime to the criminal.

Few have ever argued against the right of society to protect itself and prevent crime by detaining the criminal at least so long as there is some reason to suppose that it would be dangerous to set him free. But the right to punish anyone to deter him or others from future acts, has been widely challenged on grounds of (1) justice and (2) utility.

1. Kant and others have urged that it cannot be just to punish anyone except for a wrong actually committed; and much less can it be just to punish Peter in order to prevent Paul from attempting any crime. This is an appeal to a principle so seemingly self-evident that most writers on the criminal law have preferred to ignore the objection rather than to meet it. But modern science has made enormous progress by learning to distrust self-evident principles. We need not, therefore, hesitate to challenge Kant's assumption in this case. Why should we not inflict pain on A if that is the only way of securing the safety of the society of which he is a part, or preserving the general conditions of desirable life on which he depends for all his goods? We tax an old bachelor for the support of the education of other men's children and we conscript our youth and put them in positions where they will be killed in order that others shall be able to live. Consider the case of the typhoid carrier Mary who spreads the germs of that dreadful disease wherever she goes. Do we not by detaining her and limiting her freedom in effect punish her for her misfortune rather than for her fault? We are at all times inflicting pain on innocent people in order to promote the common good, in time of peace, as well as in war. When we need a road or bridge do we not order a family to abandon the house which has been its home from time immemorial, and for which there can be no equivalent restitution or compensation? The fact is, that the lives of individuals are not independent atoms which can be treated in isolation. We are all members

of a common body and the health of the entire body may demand inflicting pain or even the cutting off of some member.

This does not mean the complete abandonment of the principle that one should be responsible only for his own voluntary act. That would be opening the floodgates to the most extreme and outrageous injustice. But our principle may be viewed not as an isolated independent absolute, but as the statement of a general condition of the social order necessary for the good life. Certainly nothing would be more detrimental to the effective enforcement of the law than the feeling in any community that some may commit crimes for which others will be punished.

This approach comes closer to the actual conscience of humanity and cuts the ground from under the Kantian objection. A state has as much right to reform a criminal, even against his will, as to educate a child or to compel one with a contagious disease to be quarantined or to undergo curative treatment. And while it would destroy the basis of all that we hold dear in civilized life to make one man suffer merely that another be advantaged thereby, no society under present conditions can achieve the good of the whole without causing more suffering to some than to others. One need only add that we cannot be too critical in determining whether the good of the whole *is* promoted when the innocent suffer. For if we realize that our means are always part of the total end, we can see reason to doubt the goodness of an end which involves evil means. Unfortunately, however, the actual choice that life presents to any society is seldom a clear issue between absolute good and absolute evil but generally a choice between alternatives, all of which are imperfect embodiments of justice or of the highest good. Wisdom consists in such a balancing of rival considerations that the total amount of evil is minimized.

2. We come now to the much more common objection that punishment does not in fact deter either the one punished, or others. Criminals who are tempted will not, we are told, desist from taking a risk just as wolves who attack a wild horse on the Russian steppes will not abandon their effort after one or two of them are killed or crushed by the horse's hoof. There are more dangerous occupations than crime; yet people are not deterred from taking the risk.

Those who urge this objection illustrate the abuse of absolutism in the discussion of practical issues. To prove the utility of medicine it is not necessary to prove that it always prevents death and cures all instances of disease. It is enough if life is often prolonged and suffering sometimes diminished by its wise use. And to justify punishment it is not necessary to prove that it *always* prevents crime by its deterrent quality. It is enough to indicate that there would be more crime if all punishment were abolished. Now we may ignore the positivistic dogma that punishment cannot possibly have any deterrent effect, that criminals are bound to commit crimes. That kind of fatalism is not only opposed by human experience, but it is not even consistent with scientific determinism which it professes to follow. All experiments on animals as well as the historic observations of human experience indicate that fear of painful consequences is as effective a force in life as is the prospect of pleasant rewards. We are living at a time when terror on a large scale has succeeded in removing the effective temptation to rebellion. When in 1920 the police of Boston struck and left their posts, many young men broke store windows and possessed themselves of goods which they tried to sell at prices which no trained or professional criminal would demand. Sir James F. Stephen has suggested the following query: Suppose a burglar feels that he might catch a cold that would incapacitate him for as long a period as the usual prison term for burglary. Would that not deter him? Of course that largely depends on the exercise of the imagination. And the law, if wisely administered, should dramatize its punishment. It is a fact that all men live more or less in their imagination, and any imaginative realization that one will be hissed off the social stage or suffer pain is bound to act as a strong deterrent. In this connection, it is well to repeat the frequently-made, but still just, observation that not only the severity but the certainty of punishment is a factor in the case. Men will risk their lives if they think that there is some chance of winning something. And while many will take very "long" chances, as in lotteries, it is a fact that professional crime, like any other business, ceases to grow in extent when the chances of failure rise. That is why bandits do not try to rob the United States Treasury, or the Mint.

In general we know that just as certain factors will tend to increase crime, so certain factors will tend to diminish the amount of it; and that the penalties of the law, if enforced, constitute one of these minimizing causes. There is no doubt that the abolition of the police force, or the lessening of their vigilance or competence to detect the crime and to apprehend the criminal will tend to increase the amount of crime. Thus, not only the specific penalty but the question of the procedure or mechanism of its enforcement, the ease of its proof, and the likelihood of finding proper witnesses are all determinants.

It is true that men follow the *mores* apart from any fear of punishment, because normally that seems the only way in which one can act. But in a heterogeneous society, where diverse moral standards prevail and where conditions are rapidly changing, the temptation to depart from the hitherto accepted ways rises rapidly; and the fear of social disapproval decreases even more rapidly when we associate only with those who have the same inclinations that we have.

PUNISHMENT AS REPROBATION

We may look upon punishment as a form of communal expression. An organized group, like an individual, needs to give vent to its feeling of horror, revulsion or disapproval. We turn away in disgust at certain uncleanly or unaesthetic traits of an individual and exclude him from our company without inquiring as to whether it is within his power to avoid being repulsive. It is only personal love like that of a mother that can train itself to overlook repellent features or devote time and energy to eliminate them. It is *one* of the functions of the criminal law to give expression to the collective feeling of revulsion toward certain acts, even when they are not very dangerous — for example, buggery. There are, of course, various forms and degrees of social disapproval, and it is not always necessary to bring the legal machinery into operation. But at some point or other the collective feeling must be embodied in some objective communal act. By and large such expression of disapproval is a deterrent. But deterrence here is secondary. Expression is primary. Such disapproval need not be cruel or take extreme forms.. An enlightened society will recognize the futility of severely punishing unavoidable retrogression in human dignity. But it is vain to preach to any society that it must suppress its feelings. In all our various social relations — in business, in public life, in our academic institutions and even in a church — people are rewarded for being attractive and therefore penalized for not being so.

The reprobative theory will explain why it is difficult to repeal penal statutes where no one believes that the punishment will have any reformatory effect on the offender or any deterrent effect on others and consequent diminution of the number of offenses. An example of this is the law against suicide. There are also statutes such as those making adultery a crime which the community does not want to see enforced. For the publicity in the matter would do more harm than good. Yet people will not vote to repeal it; for such repeal would look like removing the social disapproval.

THE CRUELTY OF PUNISHMENT

The foregoing discussion of punishment may have impressed the reader as too hard-hearted. It seems to lack indignation at the demoralizing effect of cruelty. If punishment means inflicting pain, how can we avoid cruelty? It is no answer to say that the physician also inflicts pain, and is justified by the fact that he removes a greater amount of pain. For who can say that prison life saves the convict from more pain than it inflicts on him? Few prisoners will answer in the affirmative, for very few want to remain longer than they possibly can help. But people do go voluntarily to the doctor. No, the justification of punishment is not saving pain to the criminal but to the great mass of people who have to be protected from criminal acts.

And here it is well to note that it is impossible to live at all without inflicting pain on others as well as on one's self and on those we love. On the biological level, it is impossible to live at all without killing other creatures (plants or animals), either for purposes of food or for protection (wild beasts, vermin, etc.). In the human field we may wish to minimize the struggle for existence. But so long as different peoples want the same land (and only those who are especially prosperous are satisfied with their own possessions), and are not ready to give up what others more urgently need, there is bound to be war. And so long as two different parties want to control the government (which is likely to be the case so long as two men want the same office), there is bound to be political conflict and human suffering. It is a mistake to assume that human history shows a gradual but constant elimination of such suffering. It shows only a shift or change in the forms of it. It may perhaps be said that progress consists in the refinement of suffering. But such refinement is largely aesthetic and by no means eliminates cruelty. Under the circumstances, it is folly to preach love of all mankind, for mankind includes all the horrible villains whose atrocious villainies grow out of their human nature.

Indeed, there is nothing vile in human affairs that can genuinely be said to be foreign to human nature. All the sweetness and grace which makes life in its happy moments so delectable has its seamy side which cannot be hidden to an all-seeing eye. The effort to make life more decent therefore always involves a struggle against opposing forces. And in this struggle men find hatred, as well as love, tonic emotions. Indeed, we must hate evil if we really love the good. (Undiscriminating love extended to everyone is nonsense.) We must hate evil intensely if we are to fight it successfully, and we cannot hate theft, violence and fraud except when we see it embodied. It is thus impossible not to be indignant against certain criminals, or not to wish to punish them.

If civilization, however, means rationality in the elimination of needless cruelty, then our methods of punishment must certainly undergo profound changes even though they cannot cease to be punishments. Thus, it is progress if we stop branding criminals, even though we keep their records; and it would be retrogression if we went back to the whipping post, the stocks, the practice of breaking men's bones on the wheel, and the other old forms of torture. While the sterilization of certain kinds of criminals may be indicated, it may also open the gates to unlimited cruelty, as seems to have been the case in Nazi Germany.

The punishment provided by the criminal law is a sad necessity. But even if it is bitter medicine, there is no wisdom in unlimited doses of it. It is well to realize that the mere conviction of a crime brings social dishonor, and that may in some, though not in all, cases be sufficient. Thus, impeachment and removal from office does not necessarily demand subsequent imprisonment. But above all it is needlessly cruel to add to human temptation, or to make it more difficult for unfortunates to overcome the temptation, and then to punish them for it. Of course, every progressive step in civilization may add to the difficulties of adapting ourselves to the new social standards; and it may be argued that it is of the very essence of civilization that we should increase the temptation and with it the power of self-control. That might be claimed as the superiority of the West over the East in regard to sex relations. But after all civilization may be purchased at too great a price. Of what value is a civilization if it leads to physical and moral misery? May not one reverse the argument and say that only those social arrangements represent true progress which make life more serene and less tortured? So judged, many of the improvements of civilization might well be condemned. And the criminal law would offer a great deal of evidence along this line.

THE INDIVIDUALIZATION OF PUNISHMENT

Dominated by the reaction against the abstractness of the classical emphasis on equality and influenced by the prevailing tendency to think of crime as a disease, the idea has recently spread that in punishment we should pay more attention to the individual criminal rather than to the abstract crime. Just as medicine is turning from specific remedies, the same for everybody, to greater emphasis on individual diagnosis and treatment, so penologists are urging that since no given punishment has the same effect on different individuals, it would be more humane as well as realistic to make the punishment fit the criminal rather than the crime.

While this theory has elements of novelty in its formulation[9] and application, it is not altogether new in principle. Theoretically, it is but a re-assertion of the old idea of equity (*epieikia*) as the correction of the undue rigor of the law, a corrective to the injustice which results from the fact that the abstract rule cannot take into account all the specific circumstances that are relevant to the case. It assumes its simplest and oldest form in the pardoning power. Strictly speaking, the pardoning power is inconsistent with the view that punishment is an absolute duty prescribed by the moral law for all those found guilty by the proper tribunal. And the humane feeling or good sense of mankind has never in fact yielded to the Stoics, Kantians and others who had the courage of their one-sided dogmas. Some religions, indeed, make God's forgiveness His most glorious attribute.

Let us look at the matter a little more closely. Let us distinguish the pardoning power from the corrective justice exercised by a court when it frees a man because of a flaw in the evidence or procedure by which he has been condemned. When the technicalities of legal administration prevent courts from correcting such legal errors, the Chief Executive exercises the same judicial power when, after a hearing, he pardons the person convicted.

---

[9] It is sometimes formulated in an extremely nominalistic form, as if the individual could be treated apart from his universal detreminants.

There are cases of undoubted technical guilt, where the results of the strict application of abstract law are felt to be shocking to our moral sense. The abstract law cannot take difficulties and temptations into account, but a humane administration of it must if it is to keep the respect of the people. Theft is always a crime, but few of us would be shocked at the pardoning of a mother who stole food to prevent her children from starving. Nor would we feel that justice suffered if an escaped convict, like Jean Valjean, were pardoned after he had for so long shown the qualities of a good citizen as mayor of his town. On the contrary, we think the administration of justice inept if he is returned to the galleys. The pardoning power is also generally regarded as necessary or desirable in mass phenomena, as in the case of a general pardon for rebels, rioters, or whole classes of prisoners. It is generally issued in the form of a favor but it is actuated by a desire to promote good will to the government by placating discontented elements or diminishing the current amount of resentment. In the main, amnesty is like making peace with an army with which one has fought. If we have to live with people, it is well to have their good will. But if we allow such acts of wholesale pardon, we have abandoned absolute theories of punishment.

This is not the place for a thorough expose of the unsatisfactory character of "rigoristic" theories of morality which leave no room for the pardoning power. The superficial character of the sharp line between legal morality and social utility which these theories draw is seen in their attitude to statutes of limitation. According to the theory that rights and wrongs remain eternally what they are, the mere lapse of years can make no relevant difference to anyone's claims. But if we look carefully at the practical conditions of human conduct we cannot thus ignore the element of time. It would upset all human calculations and expectations, and thus make our transactions most uncertain if claims no matter how ancient and long-forgotten could suddenly be revived. Why may not then a man be freed from punishment, if the accusation or indictment has not been brought or pressed against him for a sufficiently long period? While statutes of limitations are not technically exercises of the pardoning power, they do illustrate the fact that people generally feel that a lapse of time justifies the abandonment of a punishment, just as a father is disinclined to punish a child for last year's fault.

When all this is said, it remains true that the pardoning power can be, and has been, a prolific source of injustice. We need not refer to the Texas governor who pardoned hundreds of criminals for his political advantage. There are other and subtler forms of injustice in the exercise of the pardoning power. A young man of good family is convicted. Then all sorts of good people intervene with testimonials which a less advantageously situated individual cannot get. When the rich or those who have political influence can thus "get away with murder," the general expectation of justice through law tends to disintegrate.

The power to pardon, which naturally includes the power to commute or reduce the terms of the court's sentence, is generally entrusted to the head of the state, who sometimes delegates it to an official such as the British Home Secretary. But if the mitigation of the rigor of the law is to be done intelligently and justly on the basis of thorough knowledge, should it not also be given to the judge who has heard all the evidence in the case and has had the guilty one before him? The recognition of this has led in recent years to increase the discretionary power of the judge in imposing sentence. Instead of fixing the penalties for diverse crimes, legislatures now tend to fix upper and lower limits between which the judge can determine by himself the proper sentence. He may even suspend sentence altogether in some cases, or put the guilty one on probation.

Any sentence, however, that the judge imposes, involves more or less a guess as to its effect on the character of the convict. But a board of prison officials who have had an opportunity to study the actual conduct of the prisoner ought to be in a better position to judge when he is ready to leave prison, fit to reenter the "free" world and engage in its lawful activities. On this theory are based the various forms of our parole system.

Any plausible attempt to reform something that has worked as atrociously as our prison system should have its frailties viewed with benevolent patience. Given time and experience, the new movement may overcome many of the evils which it has already manifested, such as the abuse of discretion by judges and parole boards, and the number of paroled prisoners who commit new crimes. But it is always helpful to clarify the issue by critically examining fundamental ideas.

1. The advocates of individualization of punishment should beware of overworking the analogy between crime and disease. Crime is not

the direct result of physiologic factors, but depends directly on social institutions. It is foolish to talk glibly of treating the criminal according to his individual nature, when in fact we have no means of adequately knowing it. The physician does not need to know all about a man's individual character. In his diagnosis he looks for very definite facts of a recurrent character, and once that is determined the treatment moves along a limited number of alternatives. But can any judge be honestly said to know the character of a person convicted sufficiently to determine what precise treatment is needed? Similarly with parole boards. A man's conduct in prison is not always the best indication of what he will do when released. And in point of fact prison officials can be and have been influenced by political and social pressure.

2. The ideology of individualization tends to an extremely nominalistic position. That is, it tends to forget the logical fact that we are apt to have more reliable knowledge about classes than about individuals, and that for certain purposes classes rather than individuals are relevant. If our country is invaded, we try to take measures against the invading army or armies. The treatment of individual soldiers is determined by these general policies. Of course, we may avoid the false ideology criticized here by admitting all this, and saying that the law needs more individualization of treatment than exists at present. But it is of the utmost importance not to forget that the abuse of discretion was one of the principle causes which led to the revolt expressed in the classical views on penology, a revolt that has undoubtedly done much for the humanization of the criminal law and its administration. And it would be a great calamity if this gain were frittered away by hastily conceived novelties.

THE KINDS OF PUNISHMENT

When we think of the great diversity of crimes, the paucity of our means of punishment is amazing. Death, imprisonment and money fine pretty nearly exhaust the field, just as the calomel pill and the lancet for blood letting exhausted the remedies of the old fashioned medical practice. Of course, any conviction brings social disgrace, which is a very severe punishment in some cases. Removal and disqualification for further public office is also an unusual and rather rare phenomenon. Recently we have introduced sterilization (in some of our states and in Germany), and it seems the only appropriate remedy for certain kinds of dreadful crimes. But the brutalizing effect on a community of thus disfiguring a human being is not to be lightly ignored. All proposals for whipping posts, and similar arrangements, should recall to us the struggle to get rid of the cruelty of the old forms of torture in the criminal law. It may be, as Dean Inge has suggested, that we have become too sensitive to pain, and that the decline of true aesthetic sensibility is associated with this hyperaesthesia. But if so, so much the worse for aesthetics.

The Death Penalty. Up to modern times the law seems to have had a remarkable preference for the death penalty. If a man gathers wood on the Sabbath, he should be stoned to death. If he says something insulting to his father or mother, he should be put to death. English law well into the nineteenth century made theft of anything over three shillings, six pence, a capital offense, and there was a long list of many other acts, now minor offenses, that were punishable with death. To be sure, on many occasions these penalties were not enforced in later times, but the idea that such penalties are necessary was certainly widely accepted.

According to the Kantian philosophy, the death penalty for a murderer is not simply permissible but is an absolute duty; and Kant wrote after Beccaria had maintained that the death penalty was absolutely wrong, incompatible with the basic social contract. The controversy as to the right of the state to kill a citizen for any cause whatsoever has continued ever since with considerable sentimental heat but not much illumination. Nor does it seem that the different parties can arrive at any agreement if they start with different attitudes towards the value of physical life. No one doubts that there is something horrible about killing a man or woman, and that the state should maintain the supreme value and sanctity of human life. Yet no one has consistently carried out the view that under no circumstances may a life be destroyed. Few deny the right of killing a bandit who attacks us or those dependent on us, and most people not only approve but glorify the killing on a wholesale scale of those with whom we are at war. We allow automobiles to kill over 36,000 people every year, which we well could prevent by foregoing the convenience it offers. (The argument that the automobile saves as many lives as it destroys or maims cannot be supported by reliable evidence). We also allow people to be killed by mine or factory accidents or through undernourishment, when we could prevent such killings by definite though expensive social measures. These examples suggest that our revulsion against murder is rather against direct and messy forms of it. Balzac has expressed that through the query: if you could inherit a great fortune by killing a Mandarin in China by just blinking your eye when no one could see you do it, would you do it? In any case, we do shorten human lives by economic conditions which compel men to undertake such work as housewrecking where the mortality is sometimes as high as twenty per cent per annum.

While these considerations throw doubt on the claim that the taking of life is absolutely prohibited by the moral code of all mankind, they do not support the present or any other legal system. It may be that in some cases the death penalty should be eliminated, but perhaps extended in other cases. Certainly we should minimize the public brutality involved in hanging or even in the burning which we call electrocution.

Fines. Fines, like money damages in the civil law, are frequent penalties in the criminal law and used to be even more common. Indeed, in former times the monetary value of human life was fixed by a definite tariff. This does not necessarily mean that human life was held cheap (though that may have been a factor), but that money was so dear that men sold themselves into practical slavery to acquire it. If a family lost a member through murder, it had a right to vengeance. But the loss might be made good by the tribe of the murdered giving up one individual who would either be killed to satisfy the desire for vengeance or made a slave to repair the loss. An additional laborer is under certain conditions as valuable as an additional ox, horse or the money that will buy other means of subsistence. Hence the seeming paradox of adopting a member of the murderer's family in settlement of the vengeance claim.

Today money penalties or fines in the criminal law violate our sense of justice, because they do not represent equal burdens on rich and poor. There is an old story of a nobleman who brutally assaulted a poor man, and when convicted had to pay what was to the nobleman a relatively small fine. When he smiled derisively and expressed great satisfaction at the outcome, the poor man was moved to make some uncomplimentary remark as to the justice of the legal system which encouraged such an outrage, whereupon he was adjudged in contempt of court and sent to jail, to the great detriment of his wife and children.

In brief, money damages means imprisonment for the poor and release for the rich.

Another ethical question which may be raised in regard to fines is: to whom shall the fine go — to the state or to the victim of the crime? Under the old English procedure, any private person could bring a criminal action and recover that part of the fine that did not go to the crown. But this partnership between the state and a private person for the collection of a fine seems to many not conducive to a dignified administration of justice.

Imprisonment. Imprisonment, originally a mere matter of detention until a debt be paid or a trial determined, has now become the most usual punishment for all crimes, except the lighter misdemeanors for which fines are generally collected. Its horrors so cry to heaven that no one ventures to say anything in defense of the system. Still it maintains itself because despite the various associations of benevolent men and women interested in prison reform, and the writings of psychologists and other students of penology, no practicable alternative has been worked out.

A few things stand out unmistakably: some may perhaps discount the accounts of the horrible sexual and other perverse conditions which prevail when we segregate a number of male or female criminals and deprive them of most of the humanizing influences that normally operate on us. After all, they may say, it is unfortunately true that most of these conditions exist also outside of prison walls. But no one denies that our prisons are the great schools of crime, that many who are committed for minor offenses learn from their associates more cunning and brutal ways. No one can dispute the depressing figures which show the large number of criminal offenders that have already served some prison term. The efforts of noble men to preach that imprisonment should be a preparation for the later free life come to naught, for they do not tell us how that consummation can be brought about. It is difficult to work out any plan which will actually succeed in reforming even young offenders who are sent to our reformatories. And even if we do succeed in educating prisoners and preparing them for some useful work, how can we guarantee them opportunity for employment, especially when millions of men without such blemishes on their records are out of work? While we may minimize, we cannot deny the fact that a prison record is a handicap in applying for a responsible position.

But when all this and much more is admitted, what feasible alternative have we to our prison system? Shall we shut up our prisons and let robbers, gunmen, and various fiends freely prey on innocent men, women and children? Imprisonment does prevent people from committing such outrages, at least so long as they are incarcerated. And while the deterrent effect of imprisonment may be small, it cannot, in the light of human experience, be denied or regarded as nil.

The foregoing reflections in no way militate against the effort to improve prison conditions and to help to save the human beings who get caught in the meshes of the criminal law. But it is well to realize difficulties that cannot be removed merely by good intentions. Many proposals for reform are altogether unobjectionable except for the external conditions that interfere with their effectiveness. There is obvious justice, for instance, in the proposal that the criminal be compelled to work to pay the victim of his crime for at least a part of the loss he has imposed on him. But to allow prison labor to compete with free labor would be seriously detrimental to the latter.

There is more merit in the proposal that the state should compensate the innocent victim of a wrongful conviction and imprisonment, just as wrongful fines and tax collections are refunded. But though this has been more or less successfully tried in several countries, the practical difficulties of assessing the money equivalent of all that is involved prevent the justice of this proposal from finding greater appeal.

On the whole, the problem of imprisonment and in general of punishing those who violate the law is one of the most disheartening ones that face modern civilization. It represents the breakdown of human intelligence as well as good will. It shows perhaps the ugliest phase of our human nature, even if we should attribute it all to our economic system or to any other *deus ex machina*.

The criminal law represents the pathology of civilization. But just as the study of animal pathology has illumined normal physiology, and has been helpful in physical hygiene, or just as the study of insanity has thrown light on mental processes and has been at times somewhat helpful in mental hygiene, so the study of criminality may illumine normal human motives and be helpful in bringing about just and humane social relations. The necessary condition for this study, however, is the most rigorous, intellectual integrity, the concentration on seeing the facts as they are, regardless of natural sentimental predilections. We must learn to live in an imperfect world, though we dare not relax the effort to make it better.

CHAPTER THREE

Absolutisms in Law and Morals

IN THE reaction against mechanical jurisprudence, against the complacent manipulation of legal concepts in utter disregard of the facts of social life, it is well to be on guard against throwing out the baby with the bath. Granted that traditional concepts like *rights, titles, contracts, etc.,* have been grossly abused, it ought still to be clear that without the use of concepts and general principles we can have no science, or intelligible systematic account, of the law or of any other field. And the demand for system in the law is urgent not only on theoretical but also on practical grounds. Without general ideas, human experience is dumb as well as blind.

It is important also in any intellectual enterprise to remember that there must always be a certain difference between theory and practice or experience. A theory must certainly be simpler than the factual complexity or chaos that faces us when we lack the guidance which a general chart of the field affords us. A chart or map would be altogether useless if it did not simplify the actual contours and topography which it describes. In advanced physical science all concepts and laws refer to ideal conditions which can never be completely realized. Thus the law of the lever tells us what would happen if we had an absolutely rigid body in the form of a purely geometric line, and the law of falling bodies states what would happen in a perfect vacuum. Neither of these conditions is perfectly attainable on earth. Similarly, it is not necessary that the principles or theoretic assumptions of legal science shall be found to be fully realized. No science offers us an absolutely complete account of its subject matter. It is sufficient if it indicates some general pattern to which the phenomena approximate more or less.

The subject matter of this article formed the substance of an address delivered before the Brookings Institution and subsequently published in the *University of Pennsylvania Law Review,* Vol. 84, p. 181 (1936). Reprinted by permission of the publisher.

For practical purposes any degree of approximation will do if it will lead to a greater control over nature than we should have without our ideal pattern. But for theoretic purposes we need the postulate that all divergences between the ideal and the actual will be progressively minimized by the discovery of subsidiary principles deduced from, or at any rate consistent with, the principles of our science.

From the foregoing there follows the necessity of two opposed attitudes. In the first place we must not forget that our fundamental principles are after all only assumptions; and that to persist in them despite factual evidence to the contrary may be foolhardy or Quixotic. On the other hand, we must have faith, courage, and persistence in our first principles. When the facts of experience seem to be in opposition we must not forget that what are generally regarded as facts may be only the blind assumptions of unreflective experience, and that the progress of science generally consists in showing that our theory can give a new and more adequate interpretation of the so-called facts. The Copernican astronomy naturally comes to our mind as an example of a theory that succeeds even though it seems at first to go counter to the universally observed fact of the motion of the sun around the earth. Our generation has also seen a remarkable instance of this in the way in which Einstein's theory of relativity has made its way despite what seemed to be established fact. The man who abandons a theory at the first difficulty which it encounters will never achieve anything in science. For in science as in everything else achievement depends upon the persistence which overcomes obstacles.

These reflections suggest a certain caution in attempting to refute legal theories on the ground that they do not seem to be in agreement with fact. These theories may have enough vitality to overcome the difficulties which seem to us fatal. It is, however, always relevant and useful to point out that such a theory is inadequate, that it leaves out certain necessary considerations. This is a relatively easy (though necessary) task because incompleteness is an inevitable characteristic of theory as well as of factual knowledge generally. What has been called absolutism in the intellectual realm is the confidence in our intellectual constructions which makes us refuse to consider the further qualifications necessary to make our general proposition true. This seems to be unavoidable. The process of qualification is laborious and seemingly endless. Practical needs and our vital and psychic economy demand absolute (*i. e.*, unqualified) answers, and make us cling to what sounds or seems to us simple. From this tendency it would hardly be possible to escape if it were not that diverse needs breed cravings for differing and opposing absolutisms. In confronting such opposites with each other we come to see the need of more adequate formulations. °

To illustrate this need is the task to which the following pages are devoted. While the outer form of my exposition will thus be almost entirely critical, its substance will, I hope, be found to be eirenic. I wish to follow the good scholastic method of Gratian's *Decretum* as well as Abelard's *Sic et non,* of trying to save the truth in opposing views by drawing the proper distinction which enables us to harmonize them.

I. LOGICAL PHASE OF LEGAL ABSOLUTISM

Absolutism in Definition

Let us begin by considering the vices of legal absolutism from the point of view of logic. The first manifestation of absolutism that suggests itself is the complacent assumption that there can be only one true or correct definition of any object. This assumption underlies the traditional controversies as to the nature of law and Kant's[1] famous reproach to jurists on this score. Yet on consulting any scholarly dictionary we can readily see that few words in common use have only one meaning. This should warn us that in controversies as to the proper definition of a term, the contestants, while using the same word (definiendum) may be really concerned with different things (definiens). Consider, for instance, Maine's[1a] criticism of Austin's[2] definition of law as an imperative or command of the sovereign. In substance Maine's objection is that there are communities in which there is no one who habitually issues commands that are generally obeyed, and yet conduct in them is governed by some law. Now the word *law* is, doubtless, used to denote the customs according to which the members of certain primitive communities generally conduct their lives. But this is no objection at all to Austin's analysis of the law found in classical Rome and in modern civilized states. In the latter

---

[1] KRITIK DER REINEN VERNUNFT (5th ed. 1797) 759A note.

[1a] MAINE, LECTURES ON EARLY HISTORY OF INSTITUTIONS (1875), lectures 12 and 13.

[2] I AUSTIN, LECTURES ON JURISPRUDENCE (2d ed. 1869), 15, 118, 120.

we certainly do find law-making bodies which abrogate certain customs, such as rebating or over-certification, and create new ones, such
as those connected with income tax returns. It is not necessary for my
present purpose to defend the complete adequacy of Austin's theory,
but merely to note that Maine does not really refute the given definition when he shows that the word *law* is also used in another sense
than that employed by Austin. Of course, the objects of these two
senses are connected, and one may well contend that law in Austin's
sense could not exist without law in Maine's sense, that is, that there
could be no sovereign whose orders are generally obeyed unless there
were certain more general customs actually prevailing, so that the
phenomenon to which Austin refers is thus sociologically derivative
and not primary. But while this statement may be true, those who
make it are generally guilty of the genetic fallacy of the identification
of a thing with its cause or condition. Law may be derived from custom but is obviously not identical with it. The law which is studied
in our law schools, administered in our courts and about which men
consult lawyers or agitate in the political forum for legislative changes
is not the same as custom. The late Mr. Carter, who identified law
and custom,[3] had the courage of his confusion and argued that judges
are experts in the customs of the various subjects on which they have
to rule. But no one else has taken that consequence of the theory
seriously. Yet, the failure to distinguish clearly between law and custom underlies all the assumptions of Ehrlich's *Living Law*.[4] There
are obviously many practices which actually prevail but are not recognized or enforced by the legal machinery, *e.g.*, the practice of tipping
waiters; and there are, on the other hand, laws regulating acts which
are in no significant sense customary, *e.g.*, the rules governing testamentary dispositions or equitable conversion. Indeed, legal prescriptions through legislation are necessary precisely because custom proves
inadequate to regulate our social relations satisfactorily.

Following Ehrlich, my friend Professor Llewellyn has argued with
great force that court litigation represents only the pathology of law,
the divergence from the normal practice. The converse of that proposition, however, cannot well be denied. Modern business practice is
undoubtedly moulded by past and expected court litigation, by legisla-

---

[3] CARTER, LAW: ITS ORIGIN, GROWTH AND FUNCTION (1907) 79.
[4] EHRLICH, GRUNDLEGUNG DER SOZIOLOGIE DES RECHTS, c. 21.

tive enactments and by administrative orders. That is what gives point to political struggles to control the organs of government.

Law as custom and law through deliberate legislation are thus both realities, and we cannot by an arbitrary definition disprove the existence of one or of the other. The important thing is rather to unravel their actual inter-relations, and that cannot be done by a mere definition.

It may seem rather trite, but it is important to insist that while there is an arbitrary element in all definitions, the question of their truth or correctness cannot be altogether dismissed. If we ignore the facts of actual historic usage, a definition is a resolution to use a word as a sign or symbol for a certain object and involves no necessary assumption that the object exists in nature. If we do not like a word in common use we can always invent a new one to denote the particular object we have in mind. In organizing a theoretic system such as geometry we are also free to choose our indefinables and our definitions will then vary according to this choice. We cannot, however, safely ignore the question of consistency in our use of words and this involves (1) attention to the meanings which our words in fact actually convey to our public and to ourselves and (2) the fact that definitions must serve a definite function in any scientific system.

(1) There can be no doubt that departures from general usage do lead to inconsistencies and confusion. For common usage is a habit and the resolution to use a word in a new sense is, like any other resolution, more easily made than kept. In point of fact, therefore, whenever we define a word like law, crime, marriage, person, or the like, in a manner that departs from current customary usage, we sooner or later unwittingly fall back on the common use and thus confuse the meaning of our terms. Regard, therefore, for common usage is a counsel of prudence or practical wisdom.

Unfortunately, however, common usage reflects common modes of thought which are generally vague and unprecise and often grossly inconsistent. Thus we commonly speak of legislatures passing laws and at other times assert that such a law when not enforced is not a law at all. Obviously this is, when taken literally, nonsense; and we can extricate ourselves from such positions either by making a sharp distinction between statutes and laws or by defining law independently of enforcement. In this way we are led to technical definitions which depart from common usage by introducing more precise limitations or distinctions.

(2) Definitions, while not absolutely necessary in pure mathematics, are practically indispensable in all sciences or responsible discourse. They can help us to grasp more clearly the fundamental ideas or patterns in any field of study and thus serve to create a definite point of view or perspective for the organization of our subject matter. In this respect some definitions are certainly more helpful than others.

From this point of view we must condemn all definitions of law (or of parts of it, *e. g.,* the criminal law) as that which is right, just, expresses the will of the majority, safeguards the social welfare or security, *etc.* For the historic complaints so bitterly and persistently made against the law raise issues of fact which cannot be properly disposed of by a mere definition. When any one says that an unjust law is not a law, that a legislative enactment is not a law unless it is the will of the majority, or that a provision of the criminal code is not a law if it does not in fact promote the safety of the community, he is resorting to a violent use of the words to escape the problem of considering the factual elements in the case.

The law about which we shall be concerned in what follows is that with which judges, lawyers and law schools are concerned, *i. e.,* with rules of conduct determinable by courts. That is what we commonly have in mind when we speak of the law of bankruptcy, divorce, *etc.,* in any state; and our discussion of what is involved in a definition of law is thus only an illustration or paradigm of what is involved in the definition of any legal institution of property, contract, and the like, on which actual decisions depend.

Absolute Divisions

The craving for greater simplicity and definiteness than our material naturally offers shows itself also in the desire for clear-cut absolute divisions. Now the simplest mode of division is that into two mutually exclusive parts such as we have when a line divides a surface into two mutually exclusive areas. This type of division (dichotomy) is especially prominent in the law where the aim is to narrow every issue down to a yes-or-no answer. Let me refer to one of these divisions to illustrate my general thesis, namely, that between criminal and civil law.

As regards substance and as regards procedure the civil and the criminal law overlap so that it is impossible to say with absolute precision where one begins and the other ends. As to substance, few today will venture to assert that all criminal acts involve greater moral turpitude than the frauds and other acts which constitute torts. Nor can we maintain the old view that the criminal law deals with acts which endanger the common welfare while the civil law deals with what is of interest only to private individuals. The general social interest in the maintenance of proper family relations, of proper industrial relations and the like, is certainly as great as that involved in the protection offered by large parts of the criminal law against various misdemeanors. Indeed, are not the same interests often protected in both ways, and are there not many acts which are both civil and criminal wrongs? As to the difference of procedure, it is easy enough to call certain procedures criminal and others civil, but not easy to define the difference. The layman, who generally thinks of crimes as serious felonies like murder and robbery, naturally says that criminal prosecutions are brought by officers of the state who are in duty bound to do so, whereas a private action is brought by an individual at his option. But leaving aside the classic common-law forms of private prosecution for criminal offenses and the fact that in England the Attorney General can still prosecute certain cases of tort, we still face the fact that an action for the collection of a land tax, or other obligation to the government, may take the form of a civil suit. Despite all sorts of theoretical differences, such as the different degrees of evidence required, such civil actions do not in effect differ very much from prosecutions to enforce penalties for certain misdemeanors. Nor can the sentence which results from criminal procedure be always sharply distinguished from the judgment in a civil action. To be sure, no civil action any longer terminates in death or imprisonment as the old Roman and Teutonic law often did. Yet even today, imprisonment for certain kinds of debts, for non-payment of alimony, and for contempt of court often grows out of civil procedure. Nor are the fines of the criminal law necessarily more severe than the civil damages that are frankly recognized as punitive. Consider, for instance, the triple damages paid by the Danbury union hatters under the Sherman Anti-Trust Law.[5] In some cases this meant the loss of home and all of a life's savings. Can we doubt that this was a punishment more

---

[5] Lawlor v. Loewe, 235 U. S. 523 (1915).

severe than that for many misdemeanors? Men sometimes prefer to
go to jail rather than pay certain fines, and the appointment of
receivers to take charge of one's business is sometimes regarded as
even worse.

These doubts cannot of course wipe out the direct and indirect
differences between criminal and civil actions; but the point I am
making is that the existence of such differences, like the existence of
the varieties of a species, does not necessarily establish a rigid dichotomous division. Similar considerations hold in regard to the dichotomous divisions between public and private law, between substantive
and procedural law, between judicial and administrative law.

We may carry over this distrust of dichotomous division to the
distinction between what is and what is not law. Looking at the
matter externally after the courts have decided, we can say what is
and what is not the law in the given case. But can we be so certain
as to the cases not yet decided? The actual element of uncertainty
as to what the courts will rule cannot be denied. Some English statutes
have become part of our common law, while others have been rejected
as inapplicable to American conditions. Have all such issues been
decided? There are many obsolescent statutes concerning which there
is no evidence or little evidence as to whether the courts will hold
them applicable to modern conditions. There are other situations
where doubt exists because there is no way of bringing the issue before
any tribunal competent to settle it. What is the status of the clause in
the Constitution directing Congress to apportion representation according to the latest census?[6] Is it law or is it a prescription of political
morality, like the duty or custom of a British Cabinet to resign after
an adverse vote in the House of Commons? Again where are we to
draw the line between a law and administrative order; *e. g.,* is a post
office regulation a law?

The foregoing and similar doubts indicate that while theoretically
we can and must define the law or branches of it in certain ways and
draw logical conclusions from them, the actual situation is not as
simple and as clear-cut as our dichotomous divisions make it appear.

On Self-Evident Principles

Though the majority of our lawyers deny the relevance or necessity
of any theory, it is not difficult to see that their view of the law

---

[6] U. S. CONST., Art. I, Sec. 2.

involves a set of absolutes. The principal one of these absolute assumptions is that the law is a closed or complete system of rules, so that no matter what case comes up from the hurly-burly of life, an answer can be deduced with absolute certainty from the principles embodied in statutes or in previously decided cases. This view, however, obviously ignores the fact that the law is not at any one time completed but is always being modified in the process of judicial decision. Not only is the common law what the judges have made it but this is also largely the case with our statutory law, of which constitutional law is a special instance. Gray seems to me to have shown this in an historically irrefutable way.[7] Against this it has been urged that if there is no law before the judge decides, the action of people and even of the judge is lawless; and this our critics regard as a *reductio ad absurdum*. This argument is, however, itself an illustration of logically vicious absolutism. It assumes that either there must be a complete law for every decision or else there is no law at all. But why not admit the fact that while judges are bound more or less by previous decisions, by general opinions, and by all the factors that Gray calls "sources of law", they also have after all the sovereign power of choice, and that in many cases they might have decided contrary to the way in which they actually did without their decisions ceasing to be, or to make, the law? Indeed, the arguments against Gray's position involve a confusion between formally possible and actual law. By giving the judge authority to make law there will always be law, but only after the judge decides. This clearly does not mean that actual legal decisions are so completely determined by previous law that the judge is a mere phonograph or automaton without opinions or sympathies of his own (based on his limited experience) that determine how he shall decide.

The insufficiency of the actual or existing law to determine completely all the issues that come up has been hidden by the use of certain maxims or principles as self-evident axioms. It is hard to see how we can avoid relying on such maxims if we are to start and get somewhere. Yet, on examination, they turn out to be largely illusory. Consider, for instance, the seemingly self-evident principle that no one can acquire a right by committing a wrong. Yet one who obtains

---

[7] GRAY, THE NATURE AND SOURCES OF THE LAW (R. Gray's ed., 2d ed. 1921) 170-189.

property by theft does acquire the right of possession against everyone except the owner, and even against the latter after a certain lapse of time. We think it self-evident that no government has a right to take the property of Peter and give it to Paul. That, we say, would be not only robbery but also a treacherous betrayal of trust, since government is instituted for the protection of property as well as life, *etc.* And yet we do, in fact, take property from Peter, in the form of taxation, and give it to Paul in the form of a pension or the education of his children or general public protection against typhoid; and few really think that this is unjust, although Peter may be a bachelor on principle and immune to typhoid. Our courts also speak as if legislatures cannot delegate their legislative powers, yet that is altogether unavoidable whenever laws have to be interpreted and applied in the course of administration.

The appeal to self-evident principles is part of traditional philosophy and especially of the Scotch intuitionism which has influenced legal thought in this country to a much larger extent than is generally realized. This intuitionism attempted to settle controversies by appeal to maxims as self-evident. It assumed that we know *a priori,* independently of all experience, that the axioms of Euclidean geometry are absolutely true in the physical world, just as according to Kant and the Romantic philosophers, we also know the *a priori* absoluteness of the law of gravitation, the laws of Newtonian mechanics, and the laws of other physical phenomena. In the same way it has been supposed that we know absolute rules or principles of law. But the fact that the people who agree on these principles draw different consequences from them shows that their agreement is merely verbal, that they use the same verbal form to denote different things.

The misleading appearance of definiteness in maxims may be seen historically when we remember that the framers of the Declaration of Independence with its ringing note about all men being created free and equal had no objection to slavery and that those who objected to the principle of taxation without representation continued to oppose granting the suffrage to those having less than a certain amount of property or to women who had property. Many good people today still repeat the latter principle, though they are violently opposed to allowing resident foreigners, illiterates and others the right to representation, even when the latter are taxed very heavily.

Courts frequently express indignation against class legislation and declare it unconstitutional as not offering to all the "equal protection of law." But the fact is that nearly all legislation is class legislation. Any law that begins with the statement, "Whoever does so and so," for example, steals something over the value of five shillings, obviously creates a penalty for a certain class of individuals, and protection for others. So do laws which recognize differences between men and women, between infants and adults, and the like. I suppose that those who object to class legislation object to unjust privilege. They do not wish to see certain classes of people receive advantages or disadvantages because of their position or status rather than because of what they do. But the actual effect of legislation always does benefit certain people more than others. That is unavoidable. I suppose that we shall all agree that a law debarring red-headed men from practising law would be a discrimination not relevant to any socially desirable end. But in actual cases where statutes have been declared unconstitutional as class legislation the legislature did see a very real connection between the distress of a given class and the remedy needed in that particular situation, while the courts have relied on verbal abstractions without any realization of the actual facts necessary to determine the concrete meaning of such abstractions.

Early American judges who thought it beyond the power of the legislature to take the property of A and give it to B also said it would be monstrous for a legislature to be able to declare the wife of A to be no longer his wife. But that is exactly what divorce laws do. I do not wish to argue the merits of divorce laws. I am merely calling attention to the fact that what horrifies people when abstractly stated may not horrify them in actual cases. Maxims are social coin and have a social value and vogue apart from their concrete meaning. But from the point of view of logic or semantics, it is an error to think of the meaning of a *legal proposition* as something completely independent of its consequences. The analysis of the facts in a situation is not only necessary in order to know what law is applicable, but the process of application develops the very meaning of our legal propositions.

If the foregoing embodies any truth we cannot pretend that the United States Supreme Court is simply a court of law. Actually, the issues before it generally depend on the determination of all sorts of facts, their consequences, and the values we attach to these consequences. These are questions of economics, politics, and social policy which legal training cannot solve unless law includes all social knowledge.

Consider Marshall's argument for the power of the courts to declare acts of Congress unconstitutional.[8] The argument starts from the clause that the Constitution is the supreme law of the land, and assuming it is self-evident that the Court is the sole interpreter of the law, concludes that the Court alone can decide what is constitutional. That this argument is not altogether as rigorous as it sounds may be seen from the fact that the Court has refused to decide what the Constitution means by a "republican form of government." It said in effect: "That is for Congress and the Executive to determine." Some things in the Constitution, then, though law, may be interpreted by Congress rather than by the courts. Indeed, Marshall's argument from the fact that the judges swear to obey the Constitution might well be turned against him with the query, Do not the President and the members of Congress also swear to act in accordance with the Constitution?

The pretence that every decision of the Supreme Court follows logically from the Constitution must, therefore, be characterized as a superstition. No rational argument can prove that when the people adopted the Constitution they actually intended all the fine distinctions which the courts have introduced into its interpretation. Nor can we well deny the fact that judges have actually differed in their interpretations, that Taney's was not that of Marshall, and that Brandeis' views are different from those of McReynolds. A sense of humor, if not of courtesy, would prevent a majority of the court from applying the term unreasonable to those interpretations of the Constitution by legislature and executive which seem reasonable to a minority of the court.

Nihilistic Absolutism

The foregoing and other abuses of logic in the law are in line with similar abuses in other fields which have been characterized as "vicious intellectualism." A reaction against this has naturally been provoked and has taken diverse forms. There has been the appeal to intuition, to common sense, to justice, to history, to the empirical facts of human behavior, or to the supposed facts of our sub-conscious or unconscious

---

8 Marbury v. Madison, 1 Cranch 136 (U. S. 1803).

thought. It is interesting to find some of these facts drawn from the mushroom science of psychoanalysis and other sources that will hardly stand up under any scientific or legal rules of evidence. All of these forms of anti-intellectualism, however, concern us here only to the extent that they lead to a nihilistic absolutism according to which there can be no logical certainty in the law at all. In the main this has been supported by the nominalistic dogma that there can be no law other than the actual individual judicial decisions, which have physiologic causes such as the state of digestion, *etc.,* but no logical determinants. I cannot here examine in detail the metaphysical assumptions of this dogmatic nihilism, which no one has ever carried out consistently because it is practically impossible to carry out any universal denial of the existence of universals.

I may, however, call attention to some obvious difficulties in such absolute denials. We select judges from those who have studied law and we expect them to obey it. How are we to discriminate between proper decisions and judicial tyranny or even corruption, if there are no rules at all to tell us whether the judge has acted within the law? Again, it is well to say that the judge is or should be guided by the facts in the case and not by *a priori* principles. But what does that mean? What facts we are to regard as relevant in a given case depend upon certain general conceptions or principles of connection. When we say a certain issue is to be settled empirically, that it depends upon the facts, it is always relevant to ask, In what way does it depend? If we cannot answer the last question, the problem of effective administration of the law has certainly not been solved.

The logical positivists or nihilists at times contend that they are not responsible for the popular expectation of justice or of certainty from the courts; and I am not arguing that any contention is untrue because it would be inconvenient if that were the case. It is, however, relevant to note that these realists do not believe in the consequences of their theory. They do not, and cannot, think that it would make no difference whether the judge did or did not know any law. Nor would they, I suppose, contend that everything that a judge says or does is law. If, however, certain acts of the judge are beyond his judicial power the determination of the latter is itself dependent on a legal rule determining his proper scope.

In any case, the historical fact is that the stream of judicial decisions

has a continuity, and judges in deciding actual cases are to some extent
influenced by the logical demands set by the prevailing conception of
what the law is or ought to be. The law is not in fact a completed,
but a growing and self-correcting, system. It grows not of itself but
by the interaction between social usage and the work of legislatures,
courts, and administrative officials, and even legal text writers. In
this growth the ideas which people have of what the law is and how
it *ought* to grow are not without influence, though obviously inadequate for complete control of all future decisions. The logical error of
absolutism is the same in the revolutionary as in the conservative
camp—the love of undue simplicity. Metaphysically this shows itself
in the assumption of absolute linearity of determination between universals and particulars, principles and actual decisions. But from universals alone we can not determine particulars, and the latter obviously
cannot completely determine the former.

In the historic process, there is no absolute beginning. When we
come to reflect we find ourselves thrown *in medias res*. We try to extract
from past decisions rules to guide the future ones, and we test the
appropriateness of these rules by the consequences to which they lead.
As these consequences are evaluated differently by different people,
such a process cannot rule out all differences of opinion based on
differences of experience or temperament, but if consistently carried
on it promotes greater order and understanding.

For dialectic or purely formal purposes, as in mathematical or logical considerations, we cannot dispense with absolute accuracy. When,
however, we come to descriptions of nature or prescriptions for human
conduct, we cannot attain such absolute precision and we have to
expect imperfection, though we must hold the ideal of perfection with
sufficient tenacity to realize that our actual achievement has fallen
short of it. This recognition of the necessity of the ideal and our
inability throughout time to achieve perfection, is the condition of
intellectual and moral sanity. It enables us to evaluate some concepts
as more definite than others. The concept of disorderly conduct, for
instance, is not as definite as that of usury or illegal rate of interest.
The progress of the law involves the attainment of greater definiteness
as well as greater flexibility. The problem of reconciling these two
demands is difficult and we can seldom attain perfect satisfaction. But
we have to learn to live in our imperfect world. We should not, in

the language of Tourtoulon, throw to the dogs all that is not fit for the altar of the gods.[9]

The foregoing criticism of logical absolutism in the law holds equally well of its ethical content. But before considering the latter it is well to glance briefly at the conflict between those who view the law as an ideal system and those who view it as completely in the field of natural existence.

II. THE REAL AND THE IDEAL IN THE LAW

The law of any country is imperative in that it orders people to do or refrain from doing certain things. Obvious as this may seem it has been vehemently denied by many influential jurists on diverse grounds. One such denial takes the form of the assertion that the law is only a system of hypothetical judgments as to what will follow in certain situations. This seems a typical instance of a purely verbal issue. If I have the power to evict you from my house what real difference does it make whether I order you out directly or tell my servant that he will see you to the door? Yet it is a mistake to ignore the importance of verbal differences in the law as in theology or in other vital social affairs. For different phrases have, because of their associations, different emotional tone and do not therefore equally fit the diverse temperaments which enter into social issues. Thus authoritarians naturally prefer the imperative terminology which is very distasteful to those who like to think that their work is scientific and that science deals only with facts of existence.

Be that as it may, the sharpest issue on the question of legal method or the nature of the legal system is that between those who view the law as a natural phenomenon, and those to whom it is an eternal ideal to which external human conduct ought to conform. The latter view is most emphatically expressed by Kant,[10] according to whom the law tells us not what empirically exists but what is categorically imperative on all societies at all times. Instances of such imperatives are the property right of the first occupier,[11] and the duty to execute a murderer.[12]

---

[9] TOURTOULON, PHILOSOPHY IN THE DEVELOPMENT OF LAW (Modern Legal Philosophy Series, 1922) 348.

[10] KANT, THE PHILOSOPHY OF LAW (Hastie's ed. 1887) 82 *et seq.*

[11] *Id.* at 82-83.

[12] *Id.* at 198.

We cannot here discuss the metaphysical foundations of this dualism; but from a juristic point of view it has encountered difficulties which it has not been able to overcome. None of its specific imperatives have been able to maintain their absoluteness. The right of the first occupier has become highly questionable in a society where it has relatively little application; and the whole *lex talionis* has been attacked as for the most part impossible of application and too brutal in those few cases where it can be applied. The main objection to all these imperatives is that as specific directions they are altogether arbitrary, that they take norms which happen and prevail among certain peoples at certain stages and set them up as valid everywhere for all times. Kant assumed that the conscience of all rational beings demands them. But this, like all arguments based on the authority of intuition or of unanimous consent, breaks down the moment you challenge it.

In reaction against this kind of absolutism, positivistic jurists insist that only if we restrict ourselves to the realm of factual or historic existence can our inquiry be called scientific. Therefore a science of the law must study only what is and have nothing to do with what ought to be. This leads to a difficulty which positivists generally pass over, namely the fact that the law does not declare or describe what exists, but rather commands or prescribes what should be done. The existence of a law of natural science can be refuted when we can show that a single phenomenon fails to conform to it, but a law in the juristic sense does not lose its claim or validity when any one acts in ways contrary to it. For the *validity* of such a law is a logical inference from certain recognized legal principles and as such does not depend upon people drawing it always, or in a majority of cases. If the Volstead Act[13] forbids the sale of alcoholic liquors, actual sales will not abrogate it. Whether it is law or not depends logically on whether it does or does not follow from the Eighteenth Amendment to the Constitution.

Two efforts have recently been made to face this. One is by the younger American jurists who follow Holmes' dictum[14] that the law is merely the set of predictions as to what the courts will decide. Looking at the law externally, this statement is unexceptionable, at least

---

13 41 STAT. 305 (1919), 27 U. S. C. A. Sec. 1 *et seq.* (1927).
14 Holmes, *The Path of the Law* (1897) 10 HARV. L. REV. 457-8.

in the context in which that great jurist stated it. The dictum, however, does not say anything about the law in the process of making, *i. e.*, how legal problems appear in the course of argument before a court or in the deliberations of a judge when he has to decide. For obviously the problem of the court is not to predict what it will do but how the case should be decided. This is also the problem of the systematic jurist or the critic of any particular decision. Any decision may be criticized on the ground that it is not consistent with the principles generally recognized or embodied in specific statutes or in repeated previous decisions that have created habitual expectations in the community. It would be disastrous for the progress of the law, therefore, if the dictum in question coupled with another misleading dictum,[15] that experience and not logic is the life of the law, were to lead to the neglect of the requirements of consistency in the law. It must be insisted that courts not only must decide individual cases, but must develop the legal system in such a way that people may generally know their rights and duties, what they may or may not do in recurrent situations.

As a system the law is developed through logical and technical methods of interpretation and analysis, whereby recurrent and relevant elements are recognized in the cases before us, and the decision made to fit as far as possible the reasonable expectations of those who have considered the law and the given case. It is not necessary to assert that this is what actually happens in every decision. It is sufficient for our present purpose to maintain that the actual law is not a pure chaos but is more or less systematic and hence that the ideal of logical system is an actual operative demand or imperative in the process of lawmaking by courts, jurists, and to some extent even by legislators.

A more elaborate attempt to deal with the normative element in the law is that of Kelsen,[16] who maintains a sharp distinction between existing social facts and what is logically demanded by the postulates of legal system. By isolating this element of validity from all questions of existence, Kelsen eliminates all descriptive sociology from his pure jurisprudence. To do this he has also to eliminate all human beings, the sovereign legislators, judges, administrators and legal subjects. No

---

[15] HOLMES, THE COMMON LAW (1881) 1.
[16] KELSEN, ALLGEMEINE, STAATSLEHRE (1925), particularly 16-21.

one can make law or administer it except one who is legally authorized to do so. State officials then have no existence as officials except as creations of the law. The whole sovereign state thus disappears and becomes merely a system of legal obligations. Kelsen likens this disappearance of the state from jurisprudence to the disappearance of the soul or consciousness from psychology. But Kelsen eliminates not only the soul but also the individual subjects. Like Cassirer and other Neo-Kantians he wishes to have a world of function without substance—a grin without a cat. We cannot, according to Kelsen, speak of the citizen obeying or disobeying the law. For the latter contains not orders to the individual citizen but only declarations to its officials as to what consequences follow certain acts. The law is thus not a command by any natural person or group to other human beings, but only a self-contained system of propositions.

No one who has followed Kelsen's work can help admiring his keen ingenuity and resourcefulness. He has undoubtedly done good service in piercing the shallow pretensions of positivistic sociologists who think that from a premise that is merely descriptive of what people do we can logically deduce what they should do. But his pure jurisprudence would be an altogether homeless ghost if he did not insist that all law must be positive, *i. e.,* actually prevail in an existing society. Here he involves himself in fundamental inconsistencies. Consider the case of official groups like the United States Congress, the Supreme Court, or ordinary juries that fail to carry out a specific legal provision. From his purely logical point of view, Kelsen must assert that the law is not changed when it is in fact disregarded or disobeyed by its officials. Yet, as a positivist, he cannot assert the existence of any law that does not prevail or is not applied in definite time and place. His admission that a revolution (which is a social phenomenon) may change the legal system shows the impossibility of eliminating all reference to existence from even the most abstract theory of what can significantly be called law.

From these and similar difficulties we can escape if we get rid of the nominalistic prejudice in favor of atomic facts, and recognize that in the world of reality existence and the relations which constitute its logical implications are inseparable. The law as a system is an ideal. And as an ideal it denotes not a number of existing decisions but something by which actual legal decisions can be determined and criticized. But it is also an historic reality in the sense that it is a logical determinant of the existing law, so that we can speak of the legal system of a given country, *e. g.*, of Sweden, and compare it with the legal system of another country or with that of the same country at another time. Legal system is a form or pattern which helps us to analyze, understand, and judge the official conduct of administrators, judges, and lawyers and the acts of others who are influenced by such conduct.

The foregoing considerations enable us to avoid not only the absolute dualism between an eternal ideal and a changing phenomenal order but to avoid also the Hegelian absolutism which ignores the distinction and brutally identifies the ideal with the actual.[17] Hegel does this not only by identifying the actual (Prussian) State with the absolute but by trying to reduce history to a purely logical process. Now it is doubtless true that the categories of logic are applicable to the historic process—history would be meaningless without them. But the material evidence on which we must construct our view of history is fragmentary and contains too many irrelevancies to justify absolute conclusions. Our best efforts can give us results which are only probable. We must therefore conclude that while existence and validity cannot be absolutely separated they cannot be absolutely identified. They are, like the two sides of a window pane, inseparable though never identical.

While logical relations are not, as such, events in time, our ideas of what ought to be can and do exercise effective influence. But we must remember that our ideals of what ought to be do not have corresponding objects as do our true ideas of what exists. Also the relation between acts and ideals by which they are to be judged is different from that between a physical event and its generalization. The same physical event may be governed by quite different legal norms. A box of shoes, for instance, leaves one place and arrives at my house. The physical path thus taken may be determinate; but whether I shall be obliged to pay for them or not is not thereby determined, but depends on legal norms or principles.

One may thus view the task of the law as the setting up of norms

---

[17] HEGEL, PHILOSOPHY OF MIND (Wallace's Trans. 1894) 147-159; PHILOSOPHY OF HISTORY (Sibree's Trans. 1894) 9-20, 475-477; PHILOSOPHY OF RIGHT (Dyde's Trans. 1896) 240-248, 278, 283, 313, 341-350.

to govern the world of actuality. But these norms themselves are historically conditioned. They depend upon considerations as to what happens most frequently under similar conditions and upon estimates as to the probable effects of certain regulations. In this sense we may say that the law selects certain norms or patterns of conduct and tries to repress extreme variations from them. It may be argued that in doing this we are continuing on the higher or conscious level the biologic process of natural selection. But without involving ourselves in the difficulties of the concept of natural selection when applied to social policies, we can certainly insist that law develops through conscious activity determined by reasons or ideals as to that which ought to be.

In this connection we may well take note of the classical controversy as to whether the law rests on reason or on force. It is interesting to note that the former view was pressed with the greatest vigor by the most typical English lawyer, typical in his practical distrust of system and rational theory. I mean, of course, Lord Coke. In an argument with King James—we have only Lord Coke's own report[18]—he urged that law was nothing but reason. When the King asked, "Have I not reason too?" Coke replied with the dodge that law is not natural but artificial reason acquired by studying the law of England. The reply to this was made by that great, though perhaps untypical, English philosopher, Hobbes, who observed that what Coke decided was law not because he had more reason than anyone else but because the King made him judge.[19]   Now, who is King or has the power to appoint judges and enforce their decisions is not purely a matter of reason but involves an element of force. Force is an element in all government or legal systems. It may take subtle forms. The rulers may govern in the name of God, the Constitution, the will of the people, or the interests of the proletariat. But ultimately they must be able to exert some kind of physical compulsion. At any rate, that is what they do in modern states. Hobbes put it brutally when he said that in the law, if nothing else turns up, clubs are trumps.[20] This is of course very crude, since as has often been remarked, you can do everything with bayonets except sit on them, and government must have a seat of

---

[18] *Prohibitions del Roy*, 12 Co. 63-65 (K. B. 1612).

[19] HOBBES, LEVIATHAN (4th ed. 1894) 125-6.

[20] HOBBES, ENGLISH WORKS (Molesworth's ed. 1840) 122.

authority. For the most important element in the efficient enforcement of governmental orders is that people should have the habit of obedience. This habit can be acquired by other means than bayonets. Consider, for instance, the way in which people obey priests, doctors, or their own young children, or the way in which an audience obeys the directions of a speaker or magician to look to one side of the room, to raise their hands, and the like. These psychologic influences of suggestion, of arousing awe or respect or psychologic fear, if not love, cannot be ignored in communal organization. Still, in the end some element of brute force is necessary to regulate a complex system of social relations and to remove recalcitrant obstruction.

The vice of absolutism to be eliminated here as before is the undue simplification of the issue. The anarchists say that law rests upon force and they trace all obedience to it. They admit that the policemen, the sheriffs and the militia are relatively few. But to the question how these few can control the vast majority, they answer that through superior organization and arms the ruling class can prevent effective opposition. Now it cannot be denied that a great deal of obedience to the law is brought about through sheer fear, so that when the police are away, the number of thefts and robberies increases. Moreover, conventional moral prohibitions are notoriously weaker when the temptation to deprive another of what is morally his due can be satisfied without legal hindrances. That is the very reason why some laws are created. Nevertheless, it is obviously not true that the state rests on the policeman's club or soldier's bayonet. The proof of that can be seen in the fact that if a vote were taken today in any of our states as to whether the police force should be completely abolished or not, the number who would vote for abolition would probably be negligible, despite the cry for relief from the burden of taxation. The maintenance of police and militia then rests upon the will of the great majority in point of fact. The majority may resent many of the laws as monstrously unjust, and they may tolerate others for no other reason than because they do not know how to get rid of them. And yet the whole system of laws with the necessary machinery of enforcement is felt to be a necessity. And if by some accident it disappeared overnight, it would very soon be restored. This does not mean that any system of laws is as good as any other. But it does mean that we generally obey the law not only from fear of punishment for its violation but because we prefer to live under a system involving some compulsion. There are many reasons for this preference. We may note in passing that men and women prefer to obey in most cases rather than take the trouble of thinking. We may see the situation concretely in the case of traffic laws. Do traffic laws rest on the force of the police or on the will of the people? The anarchistic theory says that either such laws are not necessary or they do not have to be enforced because it is obviously for the interest of everyone to have them and to obey them. Yet the fact is that without the police force, traffic rules, no matter how reasonable, would not be always obeyed by the very people who urged their enactment.

The truth, then, is that only the love of absolutism or undue simplicity prevents us from seeing that the actual facts fit into neither theory. Men do want the traffic laws and also want to disobey them. They are rational at certain times and realize that the demand for safety and ease of communication demands these rules be enforced and they vote taxes for such enforcement. Yet, they will occasionally be tempted to violate these laws. A realistic view of human nature need not hesitate to admit this irrationality of human nature against which we take some precautions in our rational moments. We all know that we are subject to certain temptations and if we are wise, we take care to arrange our lives so as to minimize the possibilities of such temptation.

III. ETHICAL ABSOLUTISM IN THE LAW

The relation between law and ethics cannot be adequately described either by identifying them or by saying that they are completely independent. There are obviously legal rules that are contrary to the general feeling of right and wrong in a community and yet are undoubtedly part of the law. If that were not the case, there could be no such thing as an unjust law and no protest against injustice by prophets or reformers who represent the conscience of the community. An unjust law does not cease to be a law because it is unjust, although it *ought* to cease to be a law. On the other hand, there are many rules of morality which find no support in the law. Only confusion, therefore, results from identifying the two and then on other occasions treating them as independent. This unfortunately is what we find in the decisions of our highest courts. On some occasions we are told: this is a court of law and not of social ethics. But at other times judges argue: this cannot be the law, for it would be unjust, *etc.*

Since the prevailing traditional view regards morality as consisting of authoritative and absolute rules, theories which conceive the law as part of morality thus share in the absolutistic tradition. This may be seen most clearly in its extreme form, to wit, in the Kantian view of law as a branch of Sittlichkeit, or social ethics. Just as "thou shalt not kill" is a categorical imperative to the individual, "thou shalt kill the murderer" is a categorical imperative to every organized community.[20a] The view that punishment is a matter merely of preventing crime or reforming the criminal is thus consistently characterized as an immoral evasion of the duty to punish. Similarly, does Schopenhauer condemn all equity which would soften the absolute rigor of the law.[21]

In our own country the morally absolutistic view of the law is embodied in the orthodox theory of our bills of rights and of the nature of our common law which, as has been frequently pointed out, rests on the classical theory of natural rights. The law is a body of principles laid down by nature or the author of nature. It has been revealed in the free institutions of the Anglo-Saxons since they inhabited the German forests (if not in the classical Roman law to which Grotius and others appealed). These principles are often referred to as the unwritten law, the unwritten constitution, or the law behind the law, revealed in the conscience of mankind. Only judges on the bench, however, can pronounce its specific legal consequences.

In its classical form, the theory finds few defenders today among those who call themselves political scientists, and there is an almost universal condemnation of it among our progressive thinkers. Indeed, the emphasis of legal scholarship since the French Revolution has been predominantly on the historical note, on the fact that the law changes and that therefore there cannot be any one set of rules valid for all times and for all societies.

This criticism, however, is obviously too sweeping and overreaches itself. Granted that law, like every phase of human life, changes with time, it does not follow that such changes are devoid of historical continuity. We do not lose our individual identity because we grow

---

[20a] See pp. 110-111 *infra.*

[21] 2 SCHOPENHAUER, THE WORLD AS WILL AND IDEA (Haldane & Kemp's Trans. 1896) 412-413.

older and sometimes sadder and wiser. Looking at the matter quite empirically, we should say that no matter how far back we trace legal systems, we find human nature and social organization presenting certain common patterns so that the law of family life today closely resembles in many respects the law of the Romans, Greeks, Hebrews and Egyptians, just as the fundamental relations between husband and wife, parents and children are still the same. There are variations doubtless between ancient and modern conditions. But there are also variations of family life in the United States today and it is by no means certain that the latter variations are less than the former. Nor is the rather superficial criticism of the historical school against the doctrine of natural rights conclusive when we look at the law as a body of prescriptions regulating our social life. Some of the rules of hygiene laid down by Hippocrates are still applicable today. Why not some legal rules? The adherents of the modernistic school insist upon historical relativity. There is no ideal best government, they say, valid for all societies. What is the best government depends upon local and historic circumstances. Quite so. But is it not necessary to ask: How and upon what circumstances does the ideal depend? Some people say that that government is best which works best. But what is to be the criterion as to what does work best or better than another?

The term "natural law" has been identified by Dean Pound and others with the idealized law of the time and place. Now, our ideal is, as we pointed out before, always conditioned by the circumstances under which we live. But let us note that natural law is often also an idealization of the opposite to that which prevails. Where inequality or privilege exists, natural law demands its abolition.

Pound does not sympathize with the lawyer, who, opposing the reception in this country of the English common law against strikes, argued that it is contrary to the rights of man and that considerations of this kind are more important than an historical inquiry as to the usages of ancient Romans, Britons, etc. Now, I confess at once that my sympathies are with the lawyer who argued thus. It is easier to analyze our present conditions and judge how for good or ill they are affected by certain rules than to find out what were the ancient social conditions that called for or tolerated an old law. Theoretically, however, the dilemma does not present mutually exclusive alternatives. The social value of modern rules against strikes may conceivably be illumined by historical considerations, and the understanding of ancient rules may be aided by a clear idea as to the fundamental values that the law aims to serve or ought to.

This critical attitude to the usual objections against the classical doctrine of natural rights does not of course dispose of the case, but it calls attention to the need of a closer examination of the issue.

The beginning of wisdom seems to me here as heretofore to keep in mind the distinction between that which is true generally or for the most part (which can be evidenced only by history) and that which necessarily holds always and everywhere without qualifications (which requires logical proof). Thus, the rule against lying may be viewed as a maxim to be generally observed because experience shows it to be requisite for that mutual trust without which many social relations are impossible or not worth while. Kant, however, in the retirement of his study definitely asserts it as an absolute rule: we may not tell a lie under any circumstances, not even to save a human life. This has appeared to many as the *reductio ad absurdum* of moral absolutism. Kant himself weakens his absolutism when he comes to apply it to the legal field. For he allows some exceptions to the duty to execute the murderer, and this opens the door to the doubt as to whether the number of exceptions might not be increased. Of course every proposition becomes absolute (*i. e.,* in no need of further qualifications) if it states all the conditions which will make it true. But in matters of fact, and especially in human relations, absolutely complete knowledge is unattainable. In the simpler issues of medicine, for instance, we can tell only what prevails generally, not what is absolutely true in every case. Much less are we in the position to determine the more complicated question as to what is ethically required in every concrete case. The law indeed does not attempt that. Recognizing the imperfection of its tools, it cannot hope to attain absolute justice. It serves its human purpose if it minimizes the amount of injustice in the community. Probably few if any laws fail to effect some injustice in special cases, but we are satisfied if on the average, they seem to do more good than harm. Thoughtful people do not expect absolute perfection from human effort. But we must faithfully and persistently *keep the ideal before us,* not only to incite even greater effort, but to keep us from falling into the deadening idolatry of the actual. Unfortunately most of the servitors of the law cannot escape the general human tendency to exalt their occupation and thus to set up the law as the object of supreme or absolute respect. Such respect may be useful in our routine or customary life. The law, however, is not the end of life but a means to facilitate the process of living; and it is folly to devote all of our attention to instruments. Certainly the law cannot be the supreme principle if we believe that it may be changed by the will of the people to make it more in harmony with their vital needs.

Legalism, the belief in the supremacy of law, cannot recognize the right of revolution. If the constitution is regarded as law, then a people can have no legal right to change it except in the way in which the constitution itself provides, no matter how onerous such a process may be. The logical consequence of this would have been to prevent the people of Rhode Island from ever changing their constitution or charter which contained no provision for amendment. Yet, the moral right of the people to make such a revolution is the very basis of our legal system. For the establishment of the United States Constitution was itself a revolution, *i. e.,* an illegal setting up of a new form of government. Indeed, it was legally more revolutionary than the Declaration of Independence. For in the latter the colonists claimed that the King of England had forfeited his sovereignty by committing illegal acts. But in setting up the United States Constitution as binding if three-quarters of the states accepted it—thus completely ignoring the Articles of Confederation which prescribed unanimous consent—no pretense of legality was alleged except the tacitly assumed right of the people to set up a new plan of government whenever they deemed it conducive to their general welfare.

An interesting manifestation of this absolutistic legalism is the view that the people of the United States can never amend the Constitution to deprive a state (without its consent) of its equal representation in the Senate. Never, never, no matter what conditions may arise, can unpopulated Nevada be deprived without its consent of the right of having as much representation in the United States Senate as states that have more than 100 times its population—a situation which in England before 1832 was called the "rotten borough system." But this idea that we can forever bind all future generations is an illusion which meets with the bitter mockery of history.

A distinction may well be urged between the right of the people to change their legal system, and their right to pass laws which are inherently or intrinsically unjust. This would be a purely academic issue if it were not for our prevailing assumption that our judges are the only ones qualified to tell what is due process or justice in any given social situation. I do not wish at this point to challenge a proposition which is generally discussed in an *a priori* fashion but which requires for its verification an appeal to actual instances. How many times have the people of the United States actually been saved by the judiciary from injustice at the hands of the legislature and executive? And how often have judicial interventions themselves produced injustice?

As history cannot prove any absolute rule, let us then briefly face the question as to what is justice in the law, and whether its dictates are absolutely certain as is so often assumed.

Since the dawn of history the bitter cry for justice has filled the human scene. But though in every discussion of any social question, all parties appeal to it, we rarely come across systematic attempts to answer the question, What is justice? And even in specific issues, for example, what is a just wage, a just price, a just claim to national independence, we find few attempts to clarify the fundamental principles assumed. Different parties all claim justice on their side. It has been said that the Romans never made war without making certain that justice was on their side. This did not prevent them from conquering all their neighbors. Nor did it prevent others from denouncing the Romans as unjust oppressors.

This diversity of views as to justice has bred a certain despair, that there is no such thing as justice and that the word conveys only diverse emotional opinions. But such a negative attitude is so contrary to the currents of practical life that the reaction to it intensifies the authoritarian view. The latter often takes the form of a claim to know by an immediate super-rational intuition or revelation what is absolutely right. Is there any way of avoiding this dilemma between the absolutism of denial and that of brute affirmation? I suggest that there is.

Suppose that we start with admitting that questions of justice are largely matters of opinion. Does it follow that all opinions are equally bad? Do not some opinions have a little more evidence in their favor than others? And is it not the quest of science to find evidence to enable us to choose the best available opinion? That is certainly not a view that can be rejected by those who believe that we can talk about sociology and psychology as sciences. The notion that science starts

with absolute facts cannot receive serious attention from those familiar
with the actual procedure and history of the most advanced physical
sciences. We always start with vague perceptions and hypotheses or
guesses, and progress consists largely of critical analysis of our hypotheses, deductions from them, and a constant checking of their consequences by appeal to perception (and a correction of our perception
by theoretical considerations). Now it may be objected that ethical
judgments, or judgments as to what ought to be, cannot by their very
nature be tested by any appeal to objective facts of existence or perception. That, however, is only partly true. In its nearsighted view
of what constitutes existence this objection ignores the rational element
in things which makes science possible. It is a radical error—indeed
an established superstition—to suppose that science is concerned only
with brute facts of existence. That would rule out pure mathematics
from the realm of science. The fact is that knowledge of nature or
physics becomes in a significant sense scientific only when it embodies
mathematical elements in the form of deduction from principles or
hypotheses, and these mathematical or logical elements denote relations of order of all objects. Now just as physical science may be
viewed as an effort to organize our judgments of nature into a coherent or rational system, so ethics may be viewed as an effort to organize
our moral judgments of what ought to be into a rational system. For
just as we may be mistaken as to the actual physical constitution of
things we may also be mistaken as to what ends we really think worthy
of achievement. This shows itself tragically in the bitter disappoint-
ments which we often feel when we achieve what we thought worthy
of effort. I do not therefore wish to minimize the difficulty in the
formulation of a theory of justice in the law. To apply it in actual
cases clearly presupposes all our knowledge of nature and man in his
social relations. Nevertheless, it is a task which is as unavoidable as
it is of vital importance. And those social scientists who think that
they can avoid it by restricting their view to what actually exists have
repeatedly been shown by history to be guilty of crypto-idealism, *i. e.*,
of setting up the existing forces or their own view as that which *ought*
to prevail. Clearly, therefore, we may start with theories or opinions
as to what is just, and by submitting them to the critical tests of logic
or scientific method discriminate between their more and their less
tenable elements. In this way we may not attain absolute truth, but

we can make progress at least in the clarification of our ideas.

Let us begin with the simplest conception of justice involved in the popular view of a just price, or a just wage. If we examine this closely, we find that the just thus designates the expected, the usual, or the customary and that, indeed, is in effect the answer of scholastic common sense. Now, it is easy enough to see the inadequacy of mere custom. For there are not only unjust customs, such as slavery and exploitation, but in a heterogeneous society or in one that is changing, what is just for one group at one time is not just at another time. Still, it is a mistake to leave out the elements of custom from the constitution of justice, as so many modern writers are inclined to do. This shows itself in the inability of moral philosophers to appreciate the importance of prescription. Why should anyone who has acquired property unjustly, get a good title after twenty or thirty years? The answer is that usage develops expectations and that the shock to general expectations is itself an evil.

Similarly, justice cannot be satisfactorily identified with any one abstract principle like equality, liberty, or the like. What is equal protection to employer and employee, for the powerful American Tobacco Company and the small storekeeper? We need not repeat the burning irony of Anatole France: "The law in its majesty draws no distinction but forbids rich and poor alike from begging in the streets or from sleeping in the public parks." Equality is meaningless under unequal conditions. And yet we do resent certain discriminations against us. Few of us, I imagine, really care to serve on juries or to hold public office. And yet, if a law were passed to disqualify us because of our race, religion or philosophic occupation, we should naturally resent the discrimination.

A similar analysis applies to the view that justice consists essentially in respecting human liberty or freedom. The word *liberty* has become a symbol around which have clung some of the most generous human emotions. We have been brought up to thrill with admiration at the men who say, Give me liberty or give me death. But the philosopher asks whether all those who are devoted to liberty mean the same thing. Does liberty, or freedom, for instance, involve free trade? Does it involve freedom to preach race hatred or the overthrow of all that we regard as sacred? Many who believe in liberty characterize the freedom which they are not willing to grant, as license, and they do it so often that one may be inclined to think that what we really need is less liberty and more license. Moreover, there is a confusion between the absence of legal restraint and the presence of real freedom as positive power to do what we want. The legal freedom to earn a million dollars is not worth a cent to one who has no real opportunity. It is fashionable to assert that men want freedom above all other things but a strong case may be made out for the direct contrary. Absolute freedom is just what people do not want; and to follow some leader, master, or mistress, or some cause that demands unqualified submission, is a deepfelt need. Orthodox Judaism, Islam, the Catholic Church, and Calvinism are not the only illustrations of the extent to which men feel liberated when they submit without question or qualification to authority. Consider the agonies of those in doubt as to the precise rules of etiquette. How relieved they feel when some good book or newspaper columnist tells them what to wear, how to order certain foods in public places and other conventionally accepted ways of doing things. The need for authority is the need for relief from the great burden of being in a state of freedom and having to think and to decide. It is much easier for most of us to let someone else take the responsibility and do the thinking and deciding for us.

But when all this is said, we do grow indignant and feel hurt to our very bones when the brutal dictatorship of a Mussolini or a Hitler deprives men of their right to express their views freely. Freedom, especially in its negative sense as the absence of restraint, will certainly not exhaust the content of what we mean by justice. But it is certainly an indispensable element in it.

An attempt to solve the problem of justice that seems to include all the elements is that of Plato, whose view might be summed up as saying that justice is the health of the body politic. Just as a body is healthy when every organ functions properly, i. e., to the degree that it reenforces rather than hinders the functioning of all the other organs, so a state or an act is just when it ministers to the general harmony of all social functions. A healthy heart is one that will supply enough blood to all the organs of the body, but not too much. So, a just social claim is one the satisfaction of which will make for the reenforcement of the various activities which constitute communal life. This is in harmony with the Hellenic ideal of everything according to measure.

Despite the fact that this view has been before mankind for over twenty-three centuries and has stimulated many minds throughout the ages, it has not proved altogether satisfactory. The criticisms of it are familiar but I shall refer to only two points: (1) the assumption of the commensurability of all social values, and (2) the optimistic assumption that we can attain the wisdom which will enable us by law to prevent injustice.

(1) It seems quite obvious that actual social conflicts cannot be readily settled by the Platonic formula. What, for instance, would be a just solution of the problem between Ireland and England or between the Ruthenians of Eastern Galicia and Poland? On one hand we have the principle of self-determination. Every group, we say, is entitled to express its own genius in language, religion, and political institutions. On the other hand, the need of common security, of preventing artificial economic barriers, is also essential, if men are to have real opportunities for free development. It is easy to say, let us have a free federation of independent groups. The real difficulty in the way of this is the difficulty of determining how much economic advantage should outweigh national pride. Indeed, the commensurability of human values is a will o' the wisp, so long as we have no ideas of a common unit wherewith to measure them all.

The problem of weighing or evaluating interests appears unduly simple in the utilitarian maxim of the greatest good to the greatest number. This assumes (a) that every individual is to count for one, and (b) that it is always possible to compare and measure different human goods. Both of these assumptions may well be questioned.

(a) That in a just legal system the interests of any one individual count for no more than the similar interests of any other individual is apt to appear as an eternal self-evident truth to those who accept the democratic faith. But critical reflection must note that in moral relations individuals and communities are not fungible but highly individualized. We may subscribe to the equalitarian doctrine when it is abstractly formulated. But few of us really accept the view that the welfare of four hundred million Chinese ought to outweigh the similar interests of one hundred and twenty-five million Americans. Nor can the obligation of providing employment for twenty thousand people in Arkansas take precedence over the task of providing employment for a few members of our own family in Maine. Differences of time also enter. While we recognize our obligations to the generations following us and feel that we ought not to impoverish the country which we are to leave to them, we do not feel that remotely future generations have the same claim on us as have our contemporaries, our children and immediate successors. We sometimes justify this on the ground that we do not know what the situation will be in the remote future and cannot therefore make provision for it. And there is doubtless some truth in this. We can look after the interests of others only when we can imaginatively put ourselves in their place. That is why we are generally more ready to help an individual stranger when we see him injured than to contribute to a general hospital fund. The fact remains, however, that in general we do not feel as much moral obligation to those who are remote from us in time or social grouping as we do to those with whom we can identify ourselves in some common interests. Nor can I see how it can possibly be proved that we ought not to feel that way. We cannot appeal to moral principles unless their obligatory character can be felt.

These doubts do not of course do away completely with the principle that where all other considerations are equal the interests of the larger number ought to prevail. Unequal distribution of wealth is generally felt to be unjust. But note that only when formulated dialectically or hypothetically can our principle be said to have absolute claims. In actual situations no one interest can be isolated and it is always doubtful whether in fact all other interests *are* similar.

(b) Those who talk freely of measuring human interests seldom examine critically the implications of the process of measurement and the conditions under which it is feasible. The modern analysis of what is involved in the addition of magnitudes shows that it is meaningless to speak of complete measurement unless we can (α) identify a standard unit capable of indefinite repetition, (β) define some operation by which we can determine that two magnitudes are equal, and (γ) define some operation which will give meaning to the sum of two or more magnitudes. These conditions have been met neither by the old hedonists who talked glibly about a hedonistic calculus—as if there were any inherent meaning in saying that one pleasure is three times as great as another—nor by the recent social scientists who identify measurement with certain crude statistical procedures.

It may be urged that while these conditions for the measurement of extensive magnitudes are not easily met in the realm of social interests, we can and do measure pleasures as intensive quantities, by the simple test of preference. Now it may be true that the more we know about people the more we can predict their preferences, and this is even more true of groups of people. But the fact remains that human preferences are proverbially inconsistent or highly variable in time, varying according to incalculable subjective factors. When will people revolt? When they are driven to it by intolerance and oppression, say some. But others with plenty of historic instances at their command, urge that oppression degrades people and robs them of the will to assert human rights. Human preferences do not seem to be the resultants of a few simple causes, but rather of a large number, no one of which can be isolated on a large scale and measured under experimental conditions. Where we deal with fungible goods as in the realm of economics, we can measure the intensity of demand. But how much or how strong a desire for economic gain will outweigh taboos against forbidden food, working on the Sabbath, making graven images, and the like? We are inclined to expect more coherence in human purposes than is actually there, because in our intellectual craving for simplicity we attribute to human life some one all-controlling purpose, such as self-preservation or the like. But this is seen to be illusion when we remember our many preferences which lead to dissolution and death.

We need not disparage the work that has recently been done on the measurement of emotion and social attitudes. So far as it rests on psycho-physical tests, it seems in the realm of verifiability. But when we go on to the social implications of these measurements we are not on such firm ground. Most studies of this sort are statistical, generally based on the answers given to questionnaires by various selected groups such as children in the movies, students in the classroom, and the like. These groups are selected because they can be readily induced to take the trouble to supply such answers. But one can well doubt whether these replies represent any characteristic that will repeat itself with any constancy. Nor is there much evidence that the replies of other people would be the same as that of our selected group, no matter how much care we have exercised to choose at random. There will always be characteristics of our group which we do not have in mind, e. g., the particular neighborhood, social class, temporary fashion, or response to some special condition of the experiment; and our inability to eliminate the fallacy of selection vitiates all our statistical generalizations.

Justice Cardozo has suggested a rather simple hierarchy of social values, to wit: moral, economic and aesthetic, which the law should protect in the order named.[22] Does this mean that no amount of economic interest can outweigh a moral duty? That would logically follow from the absolutistic conception of morality. No community, however, no matter how enlightened, ever takes that position. This there can be no higher moral obligation for a community than to prevent whenever possible the killing of human beings. Yet, measures for the protection of life can not be free from economic scrutiny, and certain costs will always be regarded as prohibitive. It may not be amiss to note in passing that those philosophers who hold that respect for human personality is absolute and the very basis of ethics, have not generally condemned wars in which countless human beings are destroyed to defend the economic interests of their country.

It may of course be argued that moral duties are not on a par with economic interests but are rather the supreme principles which determine which of a number of conflicting social interests shall in any given case prevail. But this does not solve the difficulty of how much of economic value may be disregarded in protecting specific moral standards of family life, of public conduct, *etc.* The very idea of attaching a money value to these interests is shocking and yet the duty to husband our economic resources cannot be ignored. There are limits to the economic expense which we are willing to incur to improve the administration of justice, but we are far from having arrived at any principle to enable us to do it rationally. And since in practical life we dispose of such issues by questionable resolutions we leave dissenters entirely unconvinced.

Similarly, we may well question whether economic interests should prevail over aesthetic ones, and many today condemn the extent to which our American courts have carried this doctrine. Recent thought has come to realize that the traditional Anglo-American view dictated by our business men is based on a very superficial conception of life and social needs. Aesthetic needs are basic and grow out of our fundamental instincts which are often of greater vital urge than ordinary economic ones. Certainly a major part of humanity thinks cosmetics

---

[22] CARDOZO, THE PARADOXES OF LEGAL SCIENCE (1928) 57.

and beautiful clothes worthy of economic sacrifice, even at the expense of adequate food. If we were to accept categorically the superiority of the economic over the aesthetic, we should allow the progressive uglification of our roads as well as city streets and the subordination of the scenic beauty of Niagara to the interests of electric power. But that is hardly a self-evident requirement of justice.

For years I have followed with close interest and great hope the movement of *Interessenjurisprudenz* in France, Germany, and in this country, and I regret not to be able to see as yet any substantial progress toward the solution of the problem of determining with some degree of definiteness the relative weights which different social interests should have in the legal system. Still the effort at some kind of systematic evaluation of these interests is inescapable. The possibility of intelligent choice depends on it. Possibly we shall in the course of time be able to elaborate better technics of measurement than seems feasible to us today. But it is well to realize the difficulties in our way even when we must strain our utmost to overcome them.

(2) The second objection to the Platonic theory of justice is that it is too optimistic in its conception of the capacity of law to bring about the proper social order. Throughout history there have been those who regard it as absurd to attempt to make people better by law. The law, they say, is essentially an iniquitous thing, something which is the outgrowth of fraud and violence. The monks of the fourth century felt that way when they assumed that the union between the Christian religion and the Roman state would disappoint the hope of the world by corrupting the church. The law, they said, is the crucifixion of that ideal which frees man in his inner soul. In modern times this view of the law as necessarily a restraint or bondage permeates our revolutionary as well as our conservative ideology. Consider, for instance, the philosophy of Karl Marx. Most people think of Marx as a socialist and naturally suppose him to be in favor of an organized state and, therefore, some legal system. But if you read him carefully, you find that he agrees with the anarchists that the state is essentially evil. A state or legal order is simply the enslavement of one class by another. In his challenging book on *Political Parties*,[23] Robert Michels points out that governments are inevitably

---

[23] MICHELS, POLITICAL PARTIES (1915) 11.

oligarchic because government is a special function; and those in charge of it naturally develop special capacities and interests and put these interests first. Thus every government regards the attempt to overthrow it as the most serious of all crimes. Communist Russia in this respect follows the example of the Czarist government. Ordinary murder is a matter of eight or ten years at hard labor, but an attempt to overthrow the government is a capital offense. That is characteristic of most governments. The point that Michels makes, then, is that so long as you have government, you will always have a group that has special interests, and they will necessarily think of their special interests as more important than all others. Therefore, law will always be basically unjust, and you cannot hope to make it just so long as it is administered by human beings.

To some extent, the philosophy which existed in this country in the eighteenth and for the most part in the nineteenth century, was based upon this anarchistic conception of law and justice. John Marshall, in his life of Washington, says in effect that the mere fact "that power might be abused was a conclusive argument against its being bestowed."[24] Therefore, there was instituted a government of limited powers, so that the abuses would be limited. This is a sentiment which Mr. Shaw described some time ago when he said that the United States Constitution was based upon the anarchistic theory that the best government is that which does not function.[25] I submit that this is very largely true, historically. It was the view of Jeffersonian and Jacksonian democrats who fought against the rule by the squirearchy of the Eastern border. These backwoods farmers were discriminated against in respect of legislative representation. People living far from the seat of government in a sparsely settled land cannot expect much from government regulation. The less government, the less oppression. This philosophy of an agricultural country has been used by the great manufacturing and financial interests to oppose social legislation and it has thus remained our national philosophy. Thus when a law is declared unconstitutional most people feel that no harm has happened. There is a popular view that so long as Congress is in session and is enacting laws, the people have reason to be afraid, and when Congress is adjourned, people can rejoice. That view was frequently ex-

---

[24] 2 MARSHALL, LIFE OF WASHINGTON (2d ed. 1807) 127.
[25] N. Y. Times, April 12, 1933, at 14.

pressed by our representative national philosopher, Mr. Will Rogers. I am not here discussing the merits of this view. I merely wish to indicate the large role it has played in our history. Though it originated as a revolutionary philosophy, it has become an argument of those who wish to defend their interests against the popular will expressed in legislation.

Against this pessimistic view of the inevitable injustice of man-made law we may urge the same objection as that against other forms of absolutism or undue simplicity. In actual life the fact that different classes have conflicting interests does not prevent their also having interests in common. Even the most unjust ruler may have an identity of interest with those he rules. Santayana has put this in the form of a parable which I sometimes take the liberty to repeat in a slightly modified form.[26] Imagine a wolf cunning enough to realize that, as the supply of sheep may become rather uncertain, he had better become a shepherd. He guards the flock, leads them to green pastures, and sees to it that they multiply so that he has an abundant supply. His interest as a ruler, while antagonistic, is also intertwined and for many purposes identical with that of the ruled. And that is more or less true under nearly all forms of government. There always are differences between the interest of the ruler and the ruled but also identities.

Now it may well be urged that actual wolves have no wisdom, do not turn shepherds, and that many governors, say in Burma or imperial Rome, were no better. Still, human history shows that no government can last very long if it does not render the people some service. When governments become intolerable men cease to obey or the governor is overthrown. The actual state of society, therefore, is in fact never one of mere conflict or pure opposition but a combination of both war and peace. In time of crisis we are apt to forget the common basis of human life, the touch of nature that makes all men kin. We fight without compromise and without doubts, and if anyone suggests that the other side might have some rights that we ought at least to investigate, we regard him as an enemy or perhaps a paid agent of the other side. Under such conditions, you cannot have what is called enlightened selfishness, or reason, but only an appeal to arms, and an

---

[26] Santayana, Little Essays (Smith ed. 1920) Part 5, at 259, Essay No. 102, Origin of Tyranny.

appeal to arms is a return to an uncivil state of nature in which every
man is against the other. Such struggle may remove some evil, but
it is always destructive; and sooner or later men get tired of war, and
then they make treaties of peace. Now I submit that you can view
ordinary legislation as treaties of peace between the warring interests
of the community. In point of fact, if you watch actual legislation,
whether in Harrisburg or Albany or Springfield, what you see is that
there are various interests represented in the legislature, say the rail-
road interests, the employers or the employees, the farmers, or their
wives in the W. C. T. U. and others. Each of the various groups is
constantly pressing its claims. Others are opposing those claims, and
what actually happens is just what happens at any peace treaty. The
strongest may get the lion's share, but if the strongest group could get
everything through its own power it would have no need of any treaty.
The victor makes a treaty of peace only because it is not worth while
for him to exterminate the defeated party, i. e., the defeated party still
has some fight or resistance left, and it is deemed more economical to
make some concessions rather than endure the trouble of fighting to
wipe out the will of the defeated party. And that is what happens in
legislation. We can view the law as a series of treaties of peace, which
will be just only to the extent that the various interests are genuinely
represented.

Whether our political system does or does not give genuine representation to all is a question of political analysis into which I cannot go,
but I wish to note the fact that merely geographic representation does
not guarantee actual representation of the different elements of our
population. I would like also, in passing, to protest against the popular
confusion between representative and elective government. The
knight of the shire, who was forcibly taken by the sheriff to West-
minster to vote upon the question of taxes for the king, was not elected
by his shire, but he surely was a representative of the other knights to
the extent that when he voted taxes, he represented the interests of
all those knights who were similarly circumstanced. He voted for the
interests of the knights as far as he could. In that way he was a
representative, though he was not elected. On the other hand, men
may be elected who are not at all representative. Therefore, if you
have in mind the general improvement of the law, you must also have
in mind the ways in which the various interests of a community can

receive adequate representation.

A naturalistic view of justice as the adjustment or harmony of our interests seems to many people too materialistic. Men like Carlyle call it "pig-and-swill" morality. Justice, they say, is something divinely superior. Even thoroughgoing naturalists may admit an element of truth in the last contention, in the sense that there are enormously great differences between various interests and that in the pursuit of more immediate material interests we are in danger of sacrificing higher, i. e., more subtle and more inclusive ones. But the maxim *fiat justitia pereat mundus* shows the bankruptcy of the absolutistic conception of justice. Kant indeed defends it on the ground that a world that is unjust is not worth preserving.[27] But we may well turn this around and say that a justice that would destroy the world is surely not worth having. It would certainly not serve as a basis for any relatively permanent legal system. To kill the patient in order to follow the rules of hygiene is no more absurd than to ruin a society for the sake of observing a supposed rule of justice. Even the divinely ordained Sabbath was made for man, not man for the Sabbath.

The law is an ancient institution. As is true of other human arrangements, there are people who regard it as divine. They speak of the law as if it all emanated from Sinai. But while there may be some law that emanated from Sinai, surely that is not the origin of all the legislation that we have today, nor of all judicial decisions. On the other hand, it is equally absurd to regard all law as essentially iniquitous. Let us recognize that while pure white light and absolute darkness are abstract elements of the human scene the actual colors of life are mixtures. The problem of justice is that of cleansing the social order of its black spots. This is an endless as well as a difficult task because all we do is constantly befouled by our inevitable errors and folly. But life would be unbearable without the effort at purification.

We must also remember that whatever our ideal of substantial justice, it is obviously incomplete unless it includes the ways of bringing it about. A duty that is not executory or would be a duty only under non-existent conditions is hardly a possible ideal for the legal system. Now the process of realization must start with the actual, and it depends for its success on the extent to which we utilize the actual

---

[27] KANT, *op. cit. supra* note 10 at 196.

physical and social forces, human nature and its environment. Furthermore, there can be no just order unless there is also what I have called "formal" justice, *i. e.*, a general determination on the part of those who deal with the law to live up to its spirit, to carry out not only its literal provisions but the ideal inherent in it. Doubtless, the law will never, so long as it is administered by human beings, be free from arbitrary will and brute force. Nevertheless, it cannot function in an organized society without some rational effort at justice as an ideal harmony.

In my attempt to steer a safe course between the Scylla and Charybdis of opposing absolutisms, I am not likely to have escaped serious error and may not even have made my main points tolerably clear. This is not altogether avoidable. If we distinguish clarity from mere familiarity, we can (as Peirce[28] indicated) make our ideas clear only by working out their consequences and that is a task beyond the scope of the present occasion. Our discussion, like most recent discussion in this field, has been critical and programmatic, rather than dogmatic and constructive. Yet I venture to assert that the road I have suggested is bound to prevail precisely because it is not original or novel but expresses the essence of logical or scientific method at the basis of all rational procedure. I am reluctant to use the term scientific in this connection. It has become a fetish to many who prate about it without any more real sympathy than familiarity with the rigorous self-restraint which it imposes. But if scientific method means conscientious accuracy and adequate evidence for one's assertion, some of the modernistic tendencies in jurisprudence and contemporary social science have as long a way to go as some old-fashioned legal doctrines. The former are doubtless naturally provoked by the bland complacency with which the leaders of the American bar keep on repeating questionable propositions as if no one had ever questioned their self-evidence, very much as bad pedagogues try to dispose of questions which they cannot answer by repeating their dogmas in louder authoritative tones. But we shall not get rid of vicious absolutisms by sweeping, unguarded, and unqualified denials. The swing of the pendulum is not the way of progress. The way of understanding and wisdom requires the more difficult task of just discrimination, which is inordinately difficult

---

28 PEIRCE, CHANCE, LOVE AND LOGIC (1923) 38-59.

because it involves a check to our intellectual as well as emotional *élan vital.* True intellectual vitality, however, shows itself not in letting one's self go or in romantic dreams which come in periods of fatigue, but in that self-critical effort necessary to master our material.

It is well, therefore, before concluding, not only to recognize the natural inevitability of the craving for the absolute, but to pay tribute to its necessary function in maintaining intellectual and moral sanity. It is well to be on guard against the hardly avoidable tendency to regard our impressions as definitive truths that do not require the endless process of qualification. But although this craving for undue simplicity is a fatal snare, it is folly to try to banish absolute or rigorous logic. While all the material truths which we can achieve at any one time are necessarily incomplete or subject to the qualifications of future knowledge, our procedure must be formally rigorous. The direction and goal of our efforts must be relatively fixed if there is to be any significant race. The absolute denial of all constancy or identity in the world of change and variety would make all assertions meaningless. Those who delude themselves with the naive faith of finding refuge in "the facts" are the victims of an uncritical metaphysics which assumes that each fact of existence is complete in itself and independent of every other. In truth, however, there is always a nexus which makes things pass beyond themselves, so that when you begin with one fact and wish to explore its nature you find yourself very soon beyond your starting point dealing with abstract conditions and ideal possibilities. In any case we cannot maintain sound intellectual procedure by turning our backs on critical logic; we cannot attain clear ideas as to the nature of the factual or real world by ignoring that obstinate effort to think clearly which is the core of metaphysics; and we cannot arrive at a clear idea of what it is that we really wish to achieve without the clarified vision of the *summum bonum* which is the subject matter of critical ethics. It is doubtless possible to do good work in limited fields without the conscious pursuit of these studies in their traditional forms. It is even certain that traditional errors in these fields have caused most deplorable confusions. Yet in the end, sound methods and adequate ideas are not attained by wilfully shutting our eyes; and those who have thought that they had succeeded in this by banishing logic, metaphysics and ethics from their view of the law have merely imported them in an uncritical and unavowed form.

If reason is viewed in itself as bare logic or necessary order, it seems not only colorless and devoid of warmth but also chilling to our heart's desire. Yet, on reflection we must recognize that just as the healing art is based on a dispassionate study of physiology and pathology, so is rational organization the necessary condition of our attaining our heart's desire. Philosophy cannot by itself solve the specific problems of law and public life. That requires favorable circumstances and more empirical knowledge than the philosopher generally has at his disposal. But by our very endeavor to rise above the struggle of the market place and to cultivate a wider vision, we can soften the rigors of fanatical conflicts and thus help in a measure to bring about that peace based on understanding which is the essence of liberal civilization. Rational reflection is itself a natural expression of human energy without which human life would be brutish and devoid of outlook and genuine inspiration. It is only when law is thus seen as part of the life of reason that the ideal of just law can become a real force for genuine beneficence.

CHAPTER FOUR

Kant's Philosophy of Law

I N THE consideration of Kant's philosophic system relatively little attention is nowadays paid to his theory of law. This may be in a measure due to the fact that the *Rechtslehre*[1] (the main work explicitly and systematically devoted to this theme) shows some evidence of being a product of declining years. But the more important reason is the decline of interest in the content of classical philosophy since it has been eviscerated and reduced to a general theory of *knowledge as such*. A topic of central importance to Plato, Aristotle, St. Thomas, Hobbes, Locke, Spinoza, Hume, Kant, Fichte, and Hegel is today left entirely to lawyers who think it ought to be treated by philosophers. But though the *Critique of Pure Reason* has largely contributed to this sad outcome, little reflection is needed to show that the concept of law is fundamental to the whole body of Kantian thought, theoretic as well as practical. Not only is Kant's ethics decidedly legalistic— its supreme principle is expressed in terms of universal legislation— but his basic conception of nature is that of a system of laws not far removed from the Stoic identification of the natural and the rational, which is allied to the neo-Platonic view of Galileo, Kepler, and Newton that the book of Nature is written in mathematical terms. There are doubtless differences between the laws of external motion applicable to the sensory world and the moral law within us. But both in essence emphasize abstract and invariant uniformities. Kant's moral world is an idealized celestial mechanics in which all conduct is governed by absolute rule or regularity. And the laws of physics are in the last analysis laid down by the mind in order to make phenomena objects of rational knowledge. Thus, despite his preoccupation with mathematical physics, Kant does not really abandon the teleologic view of nature, certainly not in the organic realm; and, as regards the course of human events or history, nature is certainly legislative,

---

with definite arrangements to assure moral progress for the race.[2] "A design may be traced in the mechanical course of nature itself to elicit concord out of the very discord of men, even against their wills."[3] "Nature by the mechanism of non-moral motives secures a moral result, to wit, permanent peace."[4]

The keystone of the whole Kantian system, the point at which his theoretic and practical philosophies meet, is his doctrine of God, freedom, and immortality. Though in the *Critique of Pure Reason* the proofs in their favor are rejected, their existence is by no means denied. (The idea of God is even given a regulative use for the field of natural science.) The rejection of these proofs,[5] Kant assures us, is undertaken only to establish these transcendent realities on the basis of moral faith rather than theoretic knowledge. In the doctrine of the Summum Bonum, he undertakes the latter task.

This doctrine of the Summum Bonum, expounded in the *Critique of Practical Reason,* has been a great puzzle and stumbling stone to those who approach it from the point of view of purely individual ethics. Why, after Kant has gone to so much labor to prove that we must do our duty for duty's sake and for no other reason, does he in the end spring the demand that virtue be rewarded in accordance with "worthiness to be happy." The latter unanalyzed concept seems to be dragged in *ab extra* without any relevance to, or agreement with, Kant's other ethical ideas. But the puzzle is clarified when we take

---

1 The *Rechtslehre* is the first part of the *Metaphysik der Sitten,* published in 1797. The second edition with additions and a reply to a reviewer appeared the next year. This work was translated into English by W. Hastie as Kant's *Philosophy of Law* (Edinburgh, 1887). It is cited throughout this essay as *P.L.* Kant's other writings on this theme, viz. his *Idee zu einer allgemeinen Geschichte in weltbürgerlicher Absicht* (1784), the second and third parts of *Über den Gemeinspruch: Das mag in der Theorie richtig sein, taugt aber nicht für die Praxis* (1793), and *Zum ewigen Frieden* (1795) were translated by Hastie under the title of Kant's *Principles of Politics* (Edinburgh, 1891). It is cited as *P.P.* Cassirer's edition of Kant's collected works (Berlin, 1912-1923) is cited as *C.* and Hartenstein's (Leipzig, 1867-1868) as *H.*

2 That is the main thesis of his *Idee zu einer allgemeinen Geschichte* (see especially the third proposition), and of the essay on progress which constitutes the third part of *Über den Gemeinspruch* (see especially *P.P.* p. 71). See also the second part of *Der Streit der Facultäten* (*C.,* VII, pp. 393ff.; *H.,* VII, 395ff.).

3 *Zum ewigen Frieden, C.,* VI, p. 446; *H.,* VI, p. 427; *PP.,* p. 105.

4 *ibid., C.,* VI, p. 455; *H.,* VI, p. 435; *P.P.,* p. 116.

5 See the *Preface* to the second edition of the *Kritik der reinen Vernunft, C.,* III, p. 25; *H.,* III, pp. 24f.; N. K. Smith translation (London, 1929), pp. 29f.

into account Kant's philosophy of law, according to which it is a moral imperative that offenses be punished and worthy labor be properly rewarded. A society or universe in which this is not the case is not moral or just. No moral being having power in the distribution of happiness would give wine to the drunkard or deny to virtuous desires the means of achievement.[6] "That any one should deserve happiness and yet at the same time not participate in it cannot be consistent with the perfect volition of a rational being possessed at the same time of all power."[7] In more general terms this means the belief that the imperative ideal can be realized by human conduct in the external world of time and space. While from the point of view of individual ethics the faith in personal immortality secures the continuity of moral effort, and a personal God the efficacy of that effort, when Kant comes to consider civil society and legislation, the continued existence of the human race replaces the Immortality of the soul,[8] and Nature as Providence functions as Deity.

I do not mean to defend the cogency of Kant's doctrine of the Summum Bonum or even to give here an adequate account of it. I merely wish to indicate that in the philosophy of law we touch the nub of the whole Kantian system, to wit, how pure reason, which is the only source of moral imperatives, can be effective in the actual world of human conduct.

Law according to Kant is an essential part of morality, the part which deals with those duties that can be externally enforced.

While the lawyer deals with the existing law and its application, the philosopher is concerned with the principles by which to judge what is just and what is unjust law. The distinction, however, between the law that exists and the law that ought to be is not clearly maintained by Kant, partly out of respect for established legal institutions, partly because of the ambiguity of the word *Recht*, which means both the objective law of a state and moral right; but the more important influence is Kant's teleology and philosophy of history, according to which man's actual development realizes a moral purpose of nature.

---

[6] *Tugendlehre, C.,* VII, p. 297; *H.,* VII, p. 293.

[7] *Kritik der praktischen Vernunft, C.,* W, p. 120; *H.,* V, p. 116; Abbott, *Kant's Theory of Ethics* (New York, 1927), p. 206.

[8] "It is the intention of nature to preserve the race even if thereby it sacrifices individual volition" (*Mutmasslicher Anfang der Menschengeschichte* [1786], *C.,* IV, p. 333; *H.,* IV, p. 321).

As between the view of Shaftesbury and Adam Smith that human nature is social and sympathetic and the view of Hobbes that it is essentially bellicose, Kant has the wisdom to adopt both. Like Goethe, he regards man's self-regarding or individualistic traits as implanted by nature to make him struggle and thus make progress. Man's warring disposition makes justice impossible in a state of nature. It is therefore the duty of every individual to be a member of society in which the freedom of everyone is made compatible with the freedom of everyone else by law; and it is both the right and duty of the state to enforce law as a condition of moral life.

One may accept this as generally true, or even as a necessary proposition, without admitting that this is sufficient to determine whether any specific law has the proper moral quality. It is, therefore, well to survey briefly Kant's attempt to view the whole system of law from his philosophic point of view.

THE LAW OF PROPERTY

From Kant's definition of law (*Recht*) as "the aggregate of the conditions under which the arbitrary will of one individual may be combined with that of another according to a universal law (*Gesetz*) of freedom"[9] it follows that all law is public law, and that there can thus be no law of private property apart from the civil state.[10] Kant, however, tries to differentiate private from public law, by claiming that a provisional "law of mine and thine" exists in a state of nature though not guaranteed by any organized civil society.[11] This reveals a certain difficulty in Kant's view of the relation of natural to civil law. On the one hand, the former is necessarily to be transcended by the latter; and, on the other hand, it is to control it.[12] But this is of relatively little moment here, since the law of property is in any case a demand of pure reason.[13]

Kant does not, to be sure, frequently use the term *property*, but that is essentially what he has in mind when he speaks of "having anything external as one's own." In the main he recognizes that a property right is not a dyadic relation between a person and a thing, but a relation between one person and all others in regard to the control

---

9 *Rechtslehre (Einleitung, B)*, *C.*, VII, p. 31; *H.*, VII, p. 27; *P.L.*, p. 45.
10 *ibid.* (Sec. 8), *C.*, VII, p. 58; *H.*, VII, p. 53; *P.L.*, p. 76.
11 *ibid.* (Sec. 9), *C.*, VII, p. 59; *H.*, VII, p. 54; *P.L.*, p. 78.
12 *ibid.*, *C.*, VII, p. 25; *H.*, VII, p. 22; *P.L.*, p. 33.
13 *ibid.* (Sec. 5-7), *C.*, VII, pp. 51-8; *H.*, VII, pp. 46-53; *P.L.*, pp. 66-76.

of things. Any thing, then, is my property if I have the right to exclude you, at my pleasure, from any use of it. All civil societies must, if perpetual conflict is to be avoided, regulate the control which diverse persons may exercise over the same object. There is thus no property where there is no civil law. But if the legal order is to be just it must be based on right principles. What makes the institution of private property just?

Though Kant follows Adam Smith in viewing the labor in commodities as the basis of exchange value, he does not accept the prevalent fiction that property has its origin in the right of every man to the produce of his own labor. He assumes an original common ownership, original not in any historical sense, but in the logical sense that nothing can really become juridically mine except through the recognition of my fellow citizens,[14] and labor is not the only factor which does or should determine individual ownership. This is the justification for taxation and various restraints on the exercise of the constitutional rights of property when they are prejudicial to the public interest.[15]

Kant seems to accept the doctrine of classical antiquity that first occupancy constitutes a valid title, but there is also some hint of the theory, later developed by Hegel, that property is necessary for the development of personality, from which it would follow that every person is entitled to some property. But this Kant does not develop.

An even wider issue arises as to what things may be the objects of private property. There are obviously things which have to be excluded from the domain of private control and reserved for the use of the people as a whole, e.g., public buildings, highways, parks, etc. But what things shall be so reserved is a question on which Kant is by no means clear. By branding slavery and serfdom as immoral Kant obviously restricts the right of private property so that it may not include personalities as part of one's possession. On the other hand, he comes close to ignoring the principle of personality in his introduction of the notion of real personal rights, which enables some to treat other persons as if they were inanimate things without wills of their own.

THE LAW OF CONTRACTS

One might expect, in view of Kant's rigorous insistence on the duty of truth telling and his emphatic repudiation of the right to tell a lie

[14] ibid., C., VII, p. 64; H., VII, p. 60; P.L., p. 86.
[15] ibid., C., VII, p. 131; H., VII, p. 142; P.L., pp. 183-5.

even for the sake of humanity, that he would emphasize the sanctity
of promises and try to derive the law of contracts from it. That, however, is not the case. Kant approaches the topic of contract largely
from the point of view of rights transferred by one person to another.
The contractual right itself is strictly personal, i.e. it holds only against
the other person in the transaction. In the main Kant shows the influence of Adam Smith in emphasizing the importance of a commercial
and a money economy. Though the commercial spirit is in itself as
unsocial as that of the landed nobility,[16] he regards the moneyed class
as the most trustworthy servants of the state. Trade and commerce,
indeed, are the principal means of securing general peace, which is the
essence of a legal order in the international and cosmopolitan, as well
as in the private realm.[17] On the other hand, Kant's formalism, his
insistence on the form rather than on the substance of transactions,
prevents a consistent working out or systematic elaboration of what
is involved in the law of contract as a regulation of transactions.

THE LAW OF PERSONS

In view of the central position which respect for personality occupies
in Kant's ethical philosophy, one naturally expects a very strong position as regards the law protecting the interests of personality. But,
alas, even great philosophers announce principles which have great
emotional uplift but little definite consequences. This is sadly illustrated by the fact that Kant reduces marriage—which he regards as a
law of reason—to a mutual lease of sexual organs[19] and denies to
illegitimate children the right of existence.[19] If one of the married
persons departs, the other is entitled at any time to bring such a one
back like an errant animal or runaway slave.

The protection of the individual against undue interference upon
the part of officers of the state is foreign to Kant's mode of thought.
It did not exist in the Prussia of his day and was no part of the Roman
law. Furthermore, his conception of the rights of women was singularly unsympathetic. Others in his and even earlier days did not regard
obedience on the part of a wife as a demand of natural law.[20] The

---

16 *Anthropologie* (Sec. 87), *C.*, VIII, p. 209n.; *H.*, VII, p. 639n.
17 *Rechtslehre* (Sec. 62), *C.*, VII, pp. 159-60; *H.*, VII, pp. 170-2; *P.L.*, pp. 226-8.
18 *ibid.* (Sec. 24), *C.*, VII, p. 81; *H.*, VII, p. 76; *P.L.*, p. 110.
19 *ibid.* (Sec. 49E), *C.*, VII, pp. 143-4; *H.*, VII, p. 154; *P.L.*, p. 203.

confusion between legal and natural rights shows itself in his denial of the validity of a morganatic marriage. Why should a marriage in good faith and with proper religious sanction be invalid simply because the children cannot by law succeed to the throne? Curiously enough, despite Kant's great admiration for, and intense interest in, the works of Rousseau, he says little about the rights of children. Equally indicative of the fact that Kant was following the traditional text-books and the views of his time rather than the principle of respect for personality is the extent of the rights which he grants to a master over the persons in his service.[21]

THE CRIMINAL LAW

Kant's theory of the criminal law represents in some respect the high water mark of ethical rigorism in jurisprudence. No one has come out more emphatically for the classical retributive theory. He begins with the seemingly unassailable proposition that no one may justly be punished except for having committed a crime, and he vehemently rejects what he calls the Pharisaic maxim that it is better that *one* man should die than that the whole people should perish. "For if justice and righteousness perish, human life would no longer have any value in the world!"[22] Respect for personality means that punishment must never be administered merely as a means for promoting another good, either with regard to the criminal himself (e.g. to reform him), or to civil society (e.g. to deter others from crime). "The penal law is a categorical imperative and woe to him who creeps through the serpentine windings of utilitarianism to discover some advantage that may discharge him from the justice of punishment or even from the due measure of it!"[23]

The only just principle of punishment according to Kant is the principle of retribution—the *jus talionis*. That alone, he claims, can definitely assign both the quality and quantity of a just penalty. All other standards are wavering and uncertain. "Even if a Civil Society resolved to dissolve itself with the consent of all its members—as might be supposed in the case of a people inhabiting an island resolving to separate and scatter themselves throughout the whole world—the last murderer lying in the prison ought to be executed before the resolution

[20] *ibid* (Sec. 26), *C.*, VII, p. 82; *H.*, VII, pp. 77-8; *P.L.*, pp. 111-12.
[21] *ibid*. (Sec. 30), *C.*, VII, pp. 87-8; *H.*, VII, pp. 81-2; *P.L.*, pp. 118-20. Cf., *ibid.*, *C.*, VII, pp. 166-7; *P.L.*, pp. 238-41.
[22] *ibid*. (Sec. 49E), *C.*, VII, p. 139; *H.*, VII, p. 150; *P.L.*, p. 196.

was carried out. This ought to be done in order that every one may realize the desert of his deeds, and that bloodguiltiness may not remain upon the people."[24] The imperative that a murderer must be killed is as absolute as the imperative, "Thou shalt not kill."

There is a certain verbal nobility about these seemingly rigorous principles of justice, and it must be admitted that they have very often appealed powerfully to the conscience of mankind. Throughout the ages men have revolted most poignantly at favoritism or invidious discriminations in the law. Unequal penalties to people of different stations of life or different classes have been resented as bitterly as have been inequalities in the distribution of wealth, and perhaps even more so.

But a little more regard for human experience which Kant so cavalierly rejects in this field[25] suggests that most of Kant's assertions are as weak logically as they are defective in human sympathy and understanding. It is well to assert that no one should be punished except for a crime. But what *should* be regarded as crime? Not only does Kant offer us no satisfactory answer to this question, but one cannot find in his absolute principles that reject experience any adequate basis for such an answer. To say as he does that a crime is "any transgression of the public law which makes him who commits it incapable of being a citizen"[26] is only to indicate part of the penalty for *some* crimes (i.e. felonies). And to speak as he does elsewhere of making the punishment proportional to the internal wickedness of the criminal is to forget not only that no human being can determine the internal wickedness of another, but that, as Kant himself admits, some criminals (e.g. political ones such as the Scotch Rebels) act from honorable motives.

Against those who refuse to accept the *jus talionis* and regard it as barbaric, Kant offers us no logical or ethical reply. Logically, the *jus talionis* is meaningless in all except a few cases. For the state cannot possibly do something to the criminal which is exactly equal to that which the criminal has done. How indeed *can* a punishment equal a crime? How can a state meet fraud with fraud or inhuman brutality with like conduct without demoralizing or brutalizing its members?

---

[23] *Rechtslehre, C.*, VII, p. 139; *H.*, VII, p. 149; *P.L.*, p. 195.
[24] *ibid., C.*, p. VII, p. 141; *H.*, VII, 151; *P.L.*, p. 198.
[25] e.g., *ibid., C.*, VII, p. 170; *P.L.*, p. 243.
[26] *ibid., C.*, VII, p. 138; *H.*, VII, p. 149; *P.L.*, p. 194.

What punishment can really be equal to perjury, embezzlement, or criminal seduction? Moreover, the same term in prison, like the same fine of money, does not, as Kant himself recognizes, really mean the same amount of punishment for people of different stations and sensibilities. Above all, even where there is some sort of similarity between the offense and the punishment, as in the case of murder and capital punishment, it is by no means clear that this is always demanded by the moral sense of mankind. Indeed, there are many who feel that capital punishment is never justified and who regard Kant's reply to Beccaria as highly fallacious—certainly as inconclusive.

It is characteristic that Kant himself has not the courage of his brutal principles and makes exceptions to his absolute rule in the case of a man who kills another in a duel, and of an unwedded mother who kills her infant. Also, where the number of accomplices to a murder is so great that too many citizens will be lost, Kant allows the royal prerogative[27] to override the categorical imperative, the "eternal laws of reason which should control public justice." More serious, however, is the consideration that to be consistent Kant must regard all pardon for offenders as a violation of the moral law. But to regard all mercy or forgiveness in hard cases as a sin is surely not the universal dictate of the moral conscience.

CONSTITUTIONAL LAW

On the nature of the state and the law that should control its organization and function, there is little in Kant's writings not previously put forth by Puffendorf, Hobbes, Locke, Montesquieu, Vattel, and Rousseau. But it is instructive to analyze his position even briefly, so as to see how the jural consequences of absolutism are encased in the liberalism of the Enlightenment.

To his fundamental assumption of the moral necessity for legally organized society (in order to make real freedom possible) and the consequent right of the state to enforce its decrees, Kant joins the classical theory of sovereignty *a la* Hobbes, viz. that the supreme power or ruler in a state has only rights and no enforceable duties to his subjects. The laws of the state are to be regarded as necessary *a priori* and not as merely established by statute. From this he concludes in his characteristic absolutistic manner that under no circumstances have the subjects the right to offer active resistance or rebellion. "It is the

---

[27] *ibid.*, *C.*, VII, pp. 143-5; *H.*, VII, pp. 153-5; *P.L.*, pp. 202-5.

duty of the people to bear any abuse of the supreme ruler even though it should be considered unbearable."[28] Kant does, to be sure, grant them the right to complain or to offer passive resistance, but that right amounts to nothing at all when the ruler prohibits all complaints or any kind of passive resistance. Is not every case of disobedience an act of rebellion? And Kant carries his absolutism to the extent of forbidding any investigation into how the existing government acquired its power,[29] so that people are left utterly helpless not only against a ruler who goes beyond his just power or authority but also against a usurper who succeeds in setting up an autocracy.[30]

Clearly in this attitude to the right of revolution, Kant suffers from a confusion of moral and legal categories. Legally George Washington was a rebel and a traitor before the independence of the United States was recognized by Great Britain; and if the American Revolution had failed, he might have been hanged as was Sir William Wallace. Indeed, even the setting up of the federal constitution for the United States by a process not authorized by the Articles of Confederation was a revolutionary setting aside of a previous constitution, and therefore not in conformity with the older legal order. But what reason is there for denying to people the right to do that? The fact that revolutions sometimes succeed, or that legal systems change—not always for the worse—should have reminded Kant that no actual state or government can embody absolute right or justice, and that the question whether it is worth while to go through the terrible sufferings of a revolution to obtain a better government, is one that involves a balancing of diverse advantages and disadvantages, and is thus a question of the larger prudence or expedience.

Kant's attempt to deal with the problems of government on the basis of absolutistic arguments illustrates what has been called vicious intellectualism, but is more aptly characterized as a failure to examine the adequacy of over-hasty premises. Kant assumes that it would be a logical contradiction and therefore an absolute impossibility for any

---

[28] *Rechtslehre, C.,* VII, p. 127; *H.,* VII, p. 138; *P. L.,* p. 177.

[29] *ibid.* (Sec. 52), *C.,* VII, p. 147; *H.,* VII, p. 157; *P.L.,* p. 208; cf. also *ibid.* (Sec. 49A), *C.,* VII, p. 125; *H.,* VII, p. 136; *P.L.,* p. 174; and the concluding supplementary explanation in the second edition, *ibid., C.,* VII, p. 180; *P.L.,* p. 257.

[30] Kant maintains that all authority is from God, but history shows quite clearly that men have attained supreme legislative power by force of arms or trickery that are nearer to the ways of the devil.

constitution to provide for its own overthrow or for any resistance to the supreme ruler. But history could have shown him that he had overlooked actual historic instances to the contrary. Thus Magna, Carta actually provided for armed resistance by the barons if the king violated the law; and the Constitution of the United States explicitly provides for its own amendment and thus for complete change. In the last analysis Kant really subordinates law to the will of the monarch or ruler, and justifies it by the gratuitous and unhistorical assumption that a single individual can and must embody all the claims of the legal order.

Yet Kant does not escape the liberal influence of the Enlightenment. The attempt to treat all rights as if they were terms of a social contract leads him to condemn slavery and serfdom, to discredit hereditary aristocrary, and to urge the separation of Church and State—it is to him monstrous that people should be taxed to support a church in whose teaching they do not believe. Kant also talks about just government as republican, and lodges the legislative power in the people's representatives. But these words must not mislead us. Republican government means government by law and is thus compatible with Prussian monarchy under a practical autocrat like Frederick II. Kant is decidedly vague as to what he means by representative government. He obviously thinks of a very limited franchise with few representatives, and he ignores the fact that an elected official or legislator may be in every way unrepresentative even of those who voted for him.

As a Prussian, Kant's ultimate conception of government is that of a monarchy. The logical requirement of sovereignty—of a final authoritative word—is transformed into the necessity that it be a single person whose discretion is put above the law, e.g. in the pardoning power or the power to mitigate the death penalty. Kant distrusts aristocracies and condemns any democratic constitution as despotic.[31] His argument on the last point is rather confused, but in the end it seems to amount to the contention that if all participate in government the dissenting individual will be oppressed—as if not only minorities but even majorities were not oppressed in all forms of government. Incidentally, however, Kant also supplies the best argument for democracy when he points out that simplicity of government and obedience

---

[31] *Zum ewigen Frieden, C.*, VI, p. 437; *H.*, VI, p. 418; *P.L.*, p. 92.

are not all, that there is a need for developing citizens. And does not the conferring of power and responsibility on the many tend to develop this?

As regards the proper organization of a state, Kant quite uncritically follows Montesquieu in the tripartite division of state powers into legislative, executive, and judiciary. The legislative power should belong to the citizens, not directly but presumably through elected representatives. But apprentices, servants, women, and those whose industry is controlled by others, e.g. woodcutters, resident tutors, or plowmen, are without civil personality. They are entitled to be treated as free and equal but not as active citizens.

Kant envisages the executive power as being in the hands of a supreme ruler or monarch and insists that it be irresistible. Hence, the legislative power may remove a governor but not forcibly and under no circumstances may it punish him. The killing of a king such as Charles I or Louis XVI is a complete perversion of the principles which should regulate the relation between the sovereign and his people. But if a king commits criminal acts, why should he not be punished? If it were proved that Mary Stuart participated in the murder of her husband, why should not the categorical imperative of punishment operate in her case?

Neither the legislator nor the executive, Kant maintains, should exercise the judicial function. The latter should be assigned to magistrates specifically appointed thereto. While the natural division of labor has strengthened this view and in America this has become one of the pet dogmas of constitutionalism, it is not in fact, and it is doubtful whether it can be, consistently carried through. The legislature is ultimately the highest court to judge whether officers have or have not carried out its enactments; and the executive in enforcing the law must pass judgment as to whether a given course of conduct has or has not conformed to it.

Kant's state is what the Germans call a *Polizeistaat*, not a *Kulturstaat*. It is there merely to enforce order and is in no way concerned with helping its individual members to develop their capacities for a richer life. Each individual as a free being is to mold his own fate and the state is merely to prevent certain kinds of interference from others. Natural handicaps and even the inevitable sufferings from the maladministration of the laws do not concern Kant. Philosophically, he supports an individualism like that of Bentham, without the latter's hedonism.

Kant's distrust of the concept of happiness seems to be based on the notion that it is too vague, and that the state which tries to promote the happiness of individuals is embarking on a less certain path than the state that respects the rights of every individual. Yet Kant regards it as the duty of every individual to promote the happiness of his fellows. Is there any reason for believing that a single individual is better able to promote the happiness of his fellows than is the collective power embodied in the state? There is danger of error and of benevolent despotism in both cases, but especially grave is it in the "police state" that gives certain individuals the tremendous power which the accumulation of property involves.

In the reaction against *laissez faire* we are apt to overlook the great virtue of the legalistic view, to wit, that it treats every individual as an equal—equally entitled to the protection of the law—so that all invidious class discriminations are condemned as irrational. But though this emphasis on legal equality is necessary, it is not a sufficient condition for justice in the law. For the law of property does not merely prevent interference but actually directs the way in which the social product is distributed. It is by law and not by nature that one man can own many acres which others need for their sustenance and for which they must pay him part of their labor. It is not sufficient that legal equality be merely negative. Justice seems to require that in the distribution of goods some regard for the necessities of life on the part of all citizens should be attended to. Without adequate provision for physical sustenance, freedom is a snare and a delusion. If the lawless acts of our fellow men can interfere with our moral development, why may not their organized cooperation be helpful in that regard?

INTERNATIONAL LAW

In his conception of international relations and international law Kant's juristic philosophy is seen at its best. For here he consistently applies his fundamental principle to derive significant results of unquestioned value to mankind. If a reign of civil law is necessary to save us from the natural state of war and to make moral development possible, it follows that some form of law must govern all mankind. But as (empirical) geographic conditions prevent a universal state, this supreme objective can be brought about only by a legally organized federal union of all the states. To be effective, such a union can be constituted only by republican states, i.e. by states each of which is governed by law. For the various peoples of the world have become so interdependent that a violation of just law in one place is felt everywhere else.[32] Thus the age-long craving of mankind for universal peace is connected with the supreme principle of jurisprudence and politics. This ideal of the ages has seldom been expressed with greater logical cogency and clarity, and the fact that it was written after the outbreak of the wars of the French Revolution only indicates that the validity of an ideal is not affected by the temporary defiance of it by the warlike impulses in human nature or by ruthless governmental leaders.

In the actual elaboration, however, of the principles of international law, Kant departs from his great principle and follows the usual textbooks which formulate the European conventions as to the rights of a state to declare war, etc. Thus, though he condemns spying, he does not protest against blockades which actually starve people.

*   *   *

The foregoing survey reveals a number of difficulties which are significant not only for any judgment of Kant's philosophy but for any attempt at an adequate consideration of the issues involved.

THE RELATION OF LAW TO MORALITY

That law and morality cannot be identical is obvious from a number of considerations. There are many moral duties, e.g. truth telling, which might be enforced by law and in *some* cases are enforced, but which generally are left to individual conscience or to prevailing social approval or disapproval, because attempted legal enforcement would involve great expense to the state and many inconveniences would result from it. This, however, Kant cannot allow, because it brings in questions of expediency. On the other hand, there are legal duties which are not directly moral ones. *Culpa* or unintentional wrong does not, according to Kant himself, involve any moral guilt. Yet it does involve legal penalties. But even more serious is the fact that the

---

[32] Kant also alleges that in a state where war depends upon the consent of the citizens, the latter will be loath to vote to fight in their own person, to supply the cost of the war, to repair its damage, and to bear the burden of the resulting debt. But this empirical generalization is, alas, not borne out by the actual history of representative government.

actual law can never embody perfect justice and therefore always contains elements of injustice. Kant, as was indicated above, tends to glorify the existing law and regards it as having divine authority. But if this were true, there could be no such thing as unjust law, and the whole history of the human struggle for justice throughout the ages would be a vast error or even meaningless. And Kant is not willing to accept this consequence of his view. He insists that the right or authority of the legislator to bind others by force rests on natural or moral law. But if natural law is the justification for obedience, why should we obey laws contrary to "nature" or the principles of justice?

For a better understanding of the issue involved we must realize the difficulty not only of identifying law and morality but also of completely separating them, as has been attempted by so many positivists since the days of Thrasymachus. The law affects every phase of our life directly or indirectly, and it is intellectually impossible to avoid some judgment as to what it should and what it should not do. Moreover, to say that law is simply the arbitrary will or decree of the strongest, the sovereign, or the dominant class, is either a disguised tautology or an ignoring of obvious facts. If the strongest class means the one that succeeds in enacting the legislation, then the proposition is a mere tautology. If, however, it means that certain people are for all purposes omnipotent and the rest of the people who obey are completely helpless, then it ignores the fact that a certain amount of consent on the part of the governed always exists and is in fact necessary to make law function. It is not true that law rests only on the policeman's club and soldier's bayonet. The latter depend on the support of the people who pay taxes to maintain policemen and soldiers to protect them against disturbances of the peace within their own community or from abroad. Generally speaking, it is absurd to suppose that government rests on force alone, that everyone wants to be free from law, and only fear compels anyone to obey it. As a universal proposition this is clearly false. People in the main wish to be governed and will pay a great deal for it in the way of tolerating governmental abuses. This of course does not mean that every specific law is regarded as just. But for the most part people actually respect the main body of the law and often regard it as of divine sanction, especially so in case of constitutional law. Indeed, no legal system can operate for any considerable time unless it *is* felt to be just in large measure by a large portion of the people. We may therefore assume that every existing legal system is felt to have some moral value, but that its imperfections are tolerated because actual conditions do not make a better alternative feasible.

But this balancing of advantages and disadvantages, or for that matter any calculus of values, is ruled out by Kant because he conceives of morality as consisting of specific rules each of which is absolute in its own right.

Kant's emphasis upon the categorical imperative as the supreme principle of morals (or of obedience to the law as the supreme jural principle) must not mislead us into thinking that the specific rules are derived from it. The categorical imperative in its various forms is rather the philosopher's formulation of what it is that constitutes the specific moral character of any rule. Kant is emphatic in the belief that the philosopher cannot teach mankind its moral duties. These duties rest upon the dictates of conscience which Kant repeatedly insists are universal, clear, and absolutely certain. In other words, Kant accepts the prevailing conception of the ethics of conscience as a code of nature written on the tablet of every human mind, so that even the worst criminal never complains that his punishment is unjust.

But, quite apart from the familiar difficulties as to the variability and uncertainties of conscience, we cannot logically have a number of diverse rules each of which is absolute under conditions where there are in fact conflicts. Thus, Kant regards slavery as immoral. This would make it immoral for any one to obey a law which commands the return of a slave of his owner. For thereby the individual would be actively participating in injustice. On the other hand, if he disobeys the law he is guilty of rebellion against that which is the voice of God, etc. One may take the position that the science of ethics gives us a determinate answer as to what is our duty in every case—though that is a debatable proposition—but we clearly cannot have a system of ethics constituted by a number of independent absolute rules of the kind that Kant assumes. While therefore he is profoundly sound in insisting that law is a part of enforceable social morality, the rules which he lays down cannot be absolutely valid for all societies as well as for all individuals regardless of time, place, and circumstance.

Why does Kant take that position? Ethically, it is due to the absolute contrast which he feels between rules of morality and those of prudence which he calls expediency and which men like Aristotle regard as wisdom applied to the conduct of life. Logically, however, Kant is bound by his assumption that moral rules are absolutely imperative and cannot therefore rest on experience or history. For we must remember that to Kant experience always involves a sensory element, and there is obviously nothing in the external world directly corresponding to duty or obligation.

THE FORMAL OR *A PRIORI* ELEMENTS IN THE LAW

But how can pure reason prescribe rules dealing with men and women, living on earth under diverse conditions?

It is obvious that these rules which Kant actually regards as dictated by eternal reason may be expedient or advisable under certain conditions but by no means universally so.[33]

Consider for instance his claim that life tenure for competent officials is based on reason. We may grant that such is, under certain conditions, advisable for judges, professors, possibly priests, policemen, and others. But surely there is nothing absolute or universal about such rules; and many states, if not all, have deemed it right to depart from that rule. Whatever we may think of representative government, surely election of officials for terms of office in the legislature and elsewhere cannot be judged as opposed to immutable reason. Again, Kant assumes that reason dictates that men can transmit their titles of nobility to their wives, but not conversely. But this is obviously a purely conventional arrangement and by no means rationally necessary. Kant assumes that an hereditary monarchy is rational when it exists. Yet he admits that good will or even talent is not hereditary. These are not mere lapses which might be disregarded and yet leave Kant's fundamental attitude unchanged. The very existence of human beings under different geographic conditions and with different traditional customs is an empirical or contingent fact which cannot be deduced from pure reason, and to prescribe rules as to how they should be governed without studying their actual conditions seems as absurd as to prescribe their diet or medicines *a priori* on the basis of pure reason without any admixture of empirical knowledge.

---

[33] Kant, indeed, sometimes comes close to recognizing that his legal rules are grounded in expediency. Thus, though he condemns oaths asking God's help as superstitious (*Rechtslehre* (Sec. 40), *C.*, VII, p. 110; *H.*, VII, p. 104; *P.L.*, p. 151), he is willing to allow their use if there is no other way of getting the truth. He is also willing that the death penalty should not be applied in some cases where the threat of such penalty would not be a deterrent.

This approach to the problem reduces Kant's position to such an absurdity that one may well wonder how such a powerful mind could have been led to it even in old age.

There are, however, a number of elements which make the situation more intelligible:

(1) In the first place, we must remember that in Kant's day the assertion that mathematics and physics contained *a priori* propositions was unquestioned. In the *Introduction* to the *Critique of Pure Reason* Kant assumes that the fundamental principles of Euclidean geometry and Newtonian physics are such *a priori* principles, and the whole problem of the critical or transcendental philosophy is to explain how they are possible.

(2) To this must be added the still prevailing view that the principles of ethics are eternal and immutable, and that they are revealed clearly and unmistakably in the conscience of all mankind, so that all local and temporal differences are irrelevant.

(3) Finally, the system of jurisprudence, which Kant expounds on the basis of the text-books of modern Roman law current in his day, goes back for its language and main characteristics to the classical Greek philosophy, as applied to general human relations by the Roman jurists in the *Ius Gentium,* which became the *Ius Naturale,* and seemed for millennia to be the law of human reason.

The historical development of the nineteenth century and the wider horizon produced by the discovery of non-Euclidean geometry, or non-Newtonian mechanics, and of civilizations that are not of the classical-Christian type, have made the three foregoing assumptions indefensible. We need not exaggerate the variations of legal systems. We may admit that so long as human beings have the relatively constant traits which history and psychology reveal, certain legal arrangements will always be necessary. But such judgments are surely not free from empirical elements.

There are, however, jurists such as Stammler, Reinach, and, in part, Kelsen who still contend that jurisprudence, like ethics, is a normative science prescribing what *ought to be* and cannot possibly be deduced from any empirical or other description of *what is.* By no logically valid process can we get an *ought* into our conclusion if there is none in our premises.

This theoretic position is strengthened by the practical demand of justice that we ignore all differences such as that between rich and poor, nobles and commoners, and treat all men alike. And this is represented by the traditional symbol of justice as blindfolded. She can weigh the merits of the case but she must be blind to the persons before her. The law must be no respecter of personal differences. It is the latter aspect of the popular conscience which is the basic strength of Kant's formalism. The law must not inquire as to the content of the transaction before it. It must not be concerned, e.g., with whether either party profited by the transaction in question. It must be concerned only with the question whether each was free.[34]

The unsatisfactory character of the formalistic conception of justice in its actual workings suggests, however, that its fundamental assumptions might not be altogether satisfactory. Thus, while the principle that all men should be equal before the law seems indispensable for any theory of justice, it is hardly sufficient. Justice, to be sure, demands impartiality on the part of the judge. But does this impartiality require ignoring the specific facts of the case? We say of course not! The impartiality of the judge means only that he must not take into account those facts which the law has declared irrelevant. And surely the legislator who formulates the law justly must take into account actual conditions and differences of all sorts. There may be certain kinds of class legislation that are felt to be reprehensible but surely all general legislation sets up classes; and such class differences as those between children and adults, even though the line of separation is arbitrary, are generally recognized as necessary. Even in the purely personal realm, Kant's categorical imperative, if taken to mean, Treat every man alike as a human unit, needs to be supplemented by the polar command, Treat every man (including yourself) as unique. Mephistopheles refers to Faust as the doctor, but the Lord calls him by his individual name.

Moreover, on purely intellectual grounds the formalistic position may well be attacked as in itself empty and incapable of determining any specific jural or ethical issue. Thus, while the principle of respect for personality is one that no one is inclined to challenge or deny, we may well raise the question whether by itself it determines what should or should not be the law in any given situation. Can Kant or anyone else work out a theory of punishment for the diverse kinds of crimes

---

[34] *Rechtslehre*, (*Einleitung, B.*), *C.*, VII, p. 31; *H.*, VII, p. 27; *P.L.*, p. 45.

purely on the basis of respect for personality? What does it mean to treat every individual as an end in himself? Does it mean that a government has no right to conscript a man against his will and make him kill some fellow man in battle or be killed himself?[35] Does it mean that in building a road or bridge we may not expropriate individuals who are attached to their ancestral homes? There are many cases where the wills of different individuals come in direct conflict. Two men want the same thing and their wills cannot be harmonized at all by any human law. What the law does is to provide rules whereby in a class of cases one shall prevail over the other. In all human relations we must use others as means to attain our ends, and there does not seem to be any formal rule which will enable us to tell whether, for instance, if I ask my teacher or friend to recommend me for a given position I am or am not using him *merely* as a means. There are in any cultivated society rules of respectful address, but these are fixed by convention; and there certainly are no formal rules of immutable reason to determine the degree of respect to rulers, officials, servants, etc. In general, formalism, the emphasis upon the abstract universal relation in which all men are to be considered alike, is not a method which sharpens our sensitiveness to the diversity of claims of different individuals or social groups. Thus there is not in the Kantian system any recognition of the necessity for empirical or factual studies of the actual remediable conditions that bring about intense suffering and misery. Thus Kant, despite his principle of respect for human personality, offers us no basis for promoting humane efforts to mitigate the deplorable conditions not only of those who meet with natural misfortune but also of those who are the victims of the inevitable mistakes and acts of injustice, of which governments conducted by human beings are never free.

These consequences are hidden not only in Kant's but in other formalistic jural systems by the multiplicity of fictions which have become so current that they are treated as facts and made the basis of arguments. Thus, all sorts of invidious discriminations are justified by the false assertion that economic dependence on the will of others does not involve lack of freedom. Thus, any argument that the law as a

---

[35] The argument that the state makes the individual and has a right to dispose of him as its property certainly takes no account of the principle of respect for personality.

social contract, or in any other way, actually expresses the will of *all*[36] is an obvious falsehood, and all defenses of the law based on it are sophistical.

Kant frequently invokes the principle of contradiction to prove that certain legal arrangements are impossible, for example, that a contract of slavery is self-contradictory. But if such arrangements actually exist, they cannot be logically impossible. Thus, when Kant urges that it is impossible to have a court of equity take jurisdiction over cases of conscience, he ignores the actual existence of church courts or of the English court of chancery in its original form. The principle of contradiction cannot prove existing institutions to be impossible.

This brings us back to the fundamental issue of the whole Kantian philosophy, viz., to what extent purely rational or noumenal entities can have causal efficacy in the empirical world.

CAN METAPHYSICAL FREE-WILL
BE A FACTOR IN THE LAW?

In considering the law, it is well to remember that it deals with the outwardly or phenomenally manifested acts of human beings who are born and die and are thus creatures in time and space. The freedom which these human beings demand and which the law can protect always has a spatio-temporal locus, e.g. freedom of the body from assault or detention, or freedom from hindrances to the obtaining of the things we want, e.g. food, human companionship, or the activities of self-expression in work or play. Now these activities, like all the phenomena of human conduct (including the number of marriages), are, according to Kant's own admission, subject to the laws of natural causation. Is it at all necessary, then, in considering right or just law, to go beyond the empirical realm and consider that other kind of freedom, the transcendental or metaphysical kind? It is sometimes urged that unless men are free there is no sense in holding them responsible for any of their acts. But the legal tests as to who is responsible are always empirical; and the law like all sane activity assumes some determinism in human affairs, i.e. that certain deeds will have certain consequences. This does not dispose of the problem of transcendental free will, but it indicates that it is not necessary for the determination of what is just law in the proper organization of any

---

[36] This view Kant gets directly from Rousseau.

human society. Moreover, it might not unfairly be noted, in passing, that men like Kant and Hegel who make most of metaphysical freedom, leave us rather little of the freedom that we do care about, such as freedom from oppression by despotic rulers against whose outrages we must offer no active resistance. In any case, those who like Kant try to justify government on the basis of the transcendent freedom of the individual do so by systematic ambiguity between the noumenal and phenomenal meaning of the term. In the phenomenal realm there can be no recognition of the absolute freedom of any individual. Indeed, it might well be asked whether any kind of plurality, or rational society, of absolutely free individuals is logically possible, since the very existence of any one must in some way limit any other.

Kant assumes that transcendental freedom is necessary to explain the phenomena of the moral life. But in strict logic it cannot do so. If the moral imperative which tells me to respect human personality, or to treat everyone as an end in himself, is purely rational, it cannot decide without the aid of some sensory perception the empirical fact as to who actually has human traits.

The Kantian freedom of the will means a form of causation, quite different from the kind of causation in the natural world. In the natural world cause and effect form a series in which there is no first or last term. Cause and effect are on the same level. But in moral determination pure reason, according to Kant, is not a temporal term and yet it produces practical effects in time. How that is possible or reconcilable with the universality of natural causation (on which he always insists), we are in no way told. On the other hand, if certain acts or social arrangements are pronounced unjust because they interfere with transcendental or noumenal freedom, are we not assuming that the phenomenal world can have causal efficacy in the noumenal realm? And if there is this constant interaction between the noumenal and the temporal, how can we maintain the purely rational and non-temporal character of the former?

Many details of the Kantian jurisprudence are antiquated and many more are likely to be so very soon. But Kant's attempt at a philosophy of law is still significant. For all the intellectual currents of the eighteenth century have passed through him and have been largely deflected by him. Two of these may be mentioned here, viz. traditional pietism and the philosophy of the Enlightenment. The former regards legal and moral rules as divine in origin, categorically imperative or authoritative in form, and ascetic in content. The Enlightenment sought the origin of human institutions in reason, insisted on freedom in their forms, and on the rights of human nature in their content. Kant tried a synthesis of all these elements. That he did not succeed is shown by the history of juristic and political thought since his day. To indicate some of the reasons why he failed, is a significant enterprise for those who believe that the problem must be faced as he did, but with greater regard for the factual or empirical elements and a more critical attitude to seemingly self-evident principles.

CHAPTER FIVE

Jurisprudence
as a Philosophical Discipline

THE philosophy of law has been an integral part of the great philosophical systems; but in common with other special fields of philosophy, such as the philosophy of history, it is now with us fallen into utter neglect.[1] While general interest in it can be revived only by constructive work, which will demonstrate that this ancient field can still be cultivated to bear a rich harvest, the aim of this paper is to remove some of the ground on which the prevailing apathy in regard to this subject seems to be based.

First, let us consider the view that law is a special field requiring technical knowledge, and that only the lawyer can deal with it. This is an objection which can be brought also against the philosophy of nature, and yet many of us feel that the philosophy of nature is a legitimate field of inquiry for others as well as for technical physicists, —witness our courses on the philosophy of nature, philosophy of evolution, etc. Then again in all of our colleges philosophers teach ethics. Are we ready to admit that a man need have no special knowledge of the world to teach ethics? A philosophy of law is an indispensable part of any system of social ethics; and it may well be that a good deal of the futility of modern ethics-teaching is due to its separation from what used to be called natural law. Individual ethics seems to treat terms apart from their relations. There can be no doubt, at any rate, that the significance of most ethical issues becomes apparent only if they are writ large and made principles of social legislation.

There are signs, however, that if the prevailing tendency continues, ethics will soon cease to be a philosophical study and will be abandoned to the department of sociology, anthropology, or perhaps history It becomes, therefore, necessary to reckon with this prevailing attitude which would restrict philosophy to such formal problems as the relation of mind or thought to reality.

Read at the meeting of the American Philosophical Association, New York, December, 1912, and subsequently published in *Journal of Philosophy*, Vol. 10, p. 225 (1913). Reprinted by permission of the publisher.

The view that philosophy must keep its skirts clean of any contact with the matters of fact treated in the empirical sciences is one that the most modern schools share with the older Hegelians. But whereas the Hegelians, in their endeavor after a comprehensive rational system, went on to survey all the fields of human interest, and under the guise of deduction frequently brought forth a good deal of fruitful generalization or insight, the modern tendency has been eliminating all concrete material issues from philosophy, and has reduced it to a purely formal discipline intended to give us a formal definition of reality.[2]

This modern attitude, I have tried to show elsewhere,[3] grows out of the division of labor in our American universities, and the requirements of academic courtesy. But as nature, according to Fresnel, does not care about our analytic difficulties, it may be that the universe does not run entirely for the convenience of academic administration. Be that as it may, it can, I think, be shown that, even from the narrowest conception of philosophy, the philosophy of law is still extremely useful, and that an acquaintance with general jurisprudence would enrich our discussion and teaching of logic, epistemology, and metaphysics.

To begin with, it might be shown that many chapters in the history of philosophy are unintelligible without a knowledge of the philosophy of law. Such are, for instance, the Aristotelian and Stoic conceptions of nature and its laws, the complexion of the Leibnizian monadology, or the doctrine of the *Summum Bonum* in Kant. But this would require treatment beyond the limits of this paper. I must confine myself to more obvious points.

A. Logic.—In spite of centuries of complaints of the futility of formal logic, there seems to be no tendency to give it up,—not even on the part of its most aggressive critics like Mr. Schiller. How then can we enrich it?

Now the law is the only social institution that is mainly a deduc-

---

[1] I am referring only to the Anglo-American situation, and more particularly to the latter. In Scotland and Italy the philosophy of law has always maintained itself, and in Germany and France there is to-day a vigorous revival of interest in this subject led by such men as Stammler, Joseph Kohler, Tarde, Charmont, and Saleilles. See Vol. II. of Berolzheimer's "Rechts- und Wirtschaftsphilosophie" (now translated in the Continental Legal Philosophy Series under the title, "The World's Legal Philosophies"). *Cf.* Professor Pound, *Harvard Law Review*, Vol. XXV., pages 147-168.

[2] *Philosophical Review*, Vol. XII., pages 370 ff.

[3] *The Journal of Philosophy*, Vol. VII., pages 401 ff.

tive system, or employs predominantly the logic of subsumption. Instead, therefore, of using such elementary biologic propositions as "all men are mortal" it would seem that we could use more significant material from the realm of jurisprudence. The laws of evidence are supposed by Mill to be of the essence of logic, but neither Mill nor any other logician has thought it worth while to examine the field of jurisprudence to see how the laws of evidence have actually been worked out under the pressure of life's demands. I venture to think that few logicians would find themselves unenlightened by the reading of Thayer's "Preliminary Treatise on Evidence" and his account of the genesis of our modern rational system of legal proof. Any one who is inclined to belittle the importance of definition in a deductive system will be surprised to learn how many actual transactions of daily life depend on the definition of such terms as possession or person. Even such a time-worn, threadbare topic as the logical formation of concepts receives new vigor and importance when applied to the legal field by such writers as Korkunov.[4]

B. Epistemology and Metaphysics.—Consider how much would our controversy over the nature of truth have been enriched if, instead of our easy dichotomous division of propositions into the true and false, we had taken notice of what lawyers call legal fictions. Such propositions occur, for instance, when we say that the constitution is the will of the people, or that the judges simply declare and never make the law, or when we say that the innocent purchaser of a chattel subject to mortgage has had notice of this fact if only the mortgage is duly recorded. These propositions like the statement of the actor, "I am thy father's spirit," are not adequately characterized when we say merely that they are true or that they are false. To distinguish the sense in which they may be said to be true from the sense in which they are undoubtedly false, is a significant inquiry which seems to me to throw a great deal of light on the central problem of the new realism, viz., the problem of the categories. The study of these fictions also throws light on the nature of such scientific hypotheses as those of the ether. It is curious that the only two writers who have considered fictions, Vaihinger in his "Philosophie des Als Ob" and Von Meinong in his book on *Annahmen,* have both failed to treat of the logic of legal fictions.

---

[4] Korkunov, "General Theory of Law," section 64.

We hear a good deal nowadays about intellectualism and anti-intellectualism, and I am not sure that I understand the precise point at issue. But if intellectualism means the tendency to reify or hypostatize relational concepts, *i. e.,* treat all concepts as of unchangeable entities which are independent of any context into which they enter, then there is no field which better illustrates the trouble with this vicious kind of intellectualism than the field of law.

The end of law, the administration of justice, can not be accomplished by empiricism, *i. e.,* by letting the judge decide each case on its merits. Such a hand-to-mouth existence will not do; for people must know with some degree of certainty beforehand what they may and what they may not do. Hence judges or magistrates must, even in the absence of legislation, be bound by rules, so as to eliminate as far as possible the personal equation and make the law uniform, definite, and certain. This requirement that the law should be rational, *i. e.,* deducible from established principles, compels the law to assume the form of a deductive science. But this deduction soon becomes an end in itself and is frequently pursued in flagrant contradiction with the ends of justice. Thus there results what Professor Pound has called mechanical jurisprudence, *i. e.,* a jurisprudence in which deductions are made from concepts without taking into account the question whether changing conditions have made them no longer applicable. A distinguished jurist, Windscheid, speaks of "the ancient, never-ending dream that there is a peculiar rigid and unchangeable body of legal rules which follow from pure reason and are necessary for all times and all places."[5] It is this false intellectualism which under the guise of natural rights is in the United States to-day stifling all progressive social legislation.[6]

The most cogent argument for pragmatism or instrumentalism that I know of (I speak as a friend, not as a member of the family)

---

[5] Rectoral Address, page 7.

[6] That this vice is not exclusively modern may be seen from Aristotle's "Politics." According to the Greek law if a plaintiff claimed 20 minæ when but 18 were proved to be due him, there was no course but to find for the defendant. The proposal of Hippodamus, "a strange man," to correct this and allow a verdict for the amount proved due, does not meet with the approval of Aristotle, who adds the following gem of intellectualism: "A judge who votes acquittal decides, not that the defendant owes nothing, but that he does not owe the twenty minæ claimed." ("Pol.," II., 8. 1268 *B* 15.)

The only answer to this kind of intellectualism is to be found in legal history. See Ames, *Harvard Law Review,* Vol. XXII., page 97.

is an article by Professor Pound.[7] Professor Pound does not seem to know of any pragmatists in Columbia University, and the JOURNAL OF PHILOSOPHY, published in the same University, seems never to have noticed this or any other article of Professor Pound—a significant comment on the efficiency of our modern university organization in the making of knowledge communicable.

While law thus forcibly and vividly illustrates the dangers of intellectualism, the philosophy of law even more than the philosophy of mathematics will prove a corrective to that myopic and stingy empiricism, or sensationalism, which cannot conceive anything to be real except sensible entities that have a position in time and space. The slightest reflection on the nature of legal rights or obligations, our debts, or our property if we have any, will show that these are real in any sense in which the word real is worth anything. The contingent right of the shareholder to receive a dividend, if there will be one, may in the open market fetch more than the chairs, desks, tables, or bedposts which seem to be all the furniture at the philosopher's disposal.

These possible services of jurisprudence to philosophy may seem trifling; but is not a purely formal philosophy—O tell it not to the Philistines—a magnificent piece of trifling? The sense of it must come to all of us who receive students fresh from some laboratory exercise or from a heated discussion in political science and set them to solve the problem of the "real chair." I do not mean to belittle the importance of the patient scientific work which is now being done on these formal or logical problems. On the contrary, I regard it as of no less importance than any of the researches carried on to-day in the physical or social sciences; for philosophy has always been the intellectual instrument-maker for the sciences, or at any rate the sharpener of the weapons used in all intellectual combat. But the sharpener of tools cannot carry on his business without some knowledge of the uses to which the tools are put; or to put it in more orthodox language, the analytic work of examining and criticizing fundamental concepts and methods of science cannot be carried on without a *Weltanschauung* or at least a system of values; and in any *Weltanschauung* or system of values the philosophy of law must be an integral part.

---

7 "Mechanical Jurisprudence," 8 *Columbia Law Review*, 605-610 (1908).

There seems to be a widespread conviction to-day that philosophy can at best be only a reflection on the world and by no possibility an instrument for its reform or transformation. In the oft-quoted words of Hegel, "Philosophy cannot teach the world what it ought to be. It comes too late for that . . . The owl of Minerva takes its flight only when the shades of night are gathering."[8] The history of the Hegelian philosophy itself is the best disproof of this view. For under the form of Marxian economics, or economic history, the Hegelian dialectic has, for good or for evil, been the most powerful influence in the political life of the last fifty years, just as Benthamite individualism was the most powerful influence in shaping English law and legislation of the nineteenth century.[9]

I confess I never realized the significance of Comtean positivism until lately, when in reading the history of Mexico and of other Latin-American countries I had occasion to learn the extent to which the conflict between scholasticism and positivism had been carried into the educational, legal, and political life of those countries.[10]

We are all generally acquainted with the history of the Aristotelian and Stoic doctrine of natural law, how it was carried into Roman law and used to mitigate the rigor of slavery, how it became the intellectual weapon of the people against the claims of popes and emperors, how in the hands of Grotius it proved a powerful instrument for the mitigation of the barbarities of war, or in the hands of American judges has become a powerful influence for the defense of property against the claims of society or of the working classes.[11]

To the objection which will of course be made, that ideas have no real influence in social development, that they are merely the clothes in which the dominant interests array themselves, I can only answer dogmatically that this narrow economic interpretation of history illustrates Professor Perry's fallacy of exclusive particularity. Because economic forces do undoubtedly have a large share in deter-

---

[8] Hegel, "Philosophy of Right" (tr. Dyde), page xxx.

[9] See Wilson, "The History of Modern English Law," and Dicey, "Law and Public Opinion in England."

[10] For bibliographic references, see Velverde Tellez, "Bibliografia Filosofica Mexicana."

[11] On the history and influence of "natural law," see Pollock, "The Expansion of the Common Law," lect. 4, and *Journal of the Society for Comparative Legislation,* 1900, pages 418 ff. Under the form of the *jus gentium* it occurs even in Bracton. (De Legibus, etc., lib. I., ch. 2, fol. 9a.)

mining history it does not follow that everything else is uninfluential. One can easily point out instances in the law of trusts or partnerships where judges have been influenced by tradition, sentiment, or the exigencies of a received system even against the interests of the class which they represent.[12] The American doctrine of the independence of the judiciary, or of government by three coordinate branches, is to-day the bulwark of our economically regnant classes; but it originated as a matter of fact in certain logical considerations in Aristotle and was copied into the American Constitution, not because of any class interests, but because of the "imposing" character of the learning in Montesquieu's book on the "Spirit of Laws."

In our reaction against the old despotic claim of philosophy as the absolute ruler and dictator to all human investigation, we have gone to the other extreme and have put it in the position of a useless servant. To this servile period of philosophy there must succeed a period of genuine cooperation between philosophy and the special sciences. This cooperation is becoming easier because the various sciences are beginning to outgrow their juvenile fear of philosophy. and are no longer so effectively frightened by the bogey of metaphysics. This is happening not only in mathematics, physics, chemistry, and biology,—witness Russell, Poincaré, Duhem, Ostwald, Driesch, and others—but also in jurisprudence.

When, under the influence of British empiricism, conscious philosophy of law was almost ridiculed out of existence, the door was left open for the antiquated individualistic natural rights philosophy of the eighteenth century, as embodied in text-books like Blackstone. As narrow empiricism always terminates in vicious intellectualism, so the pseudo-philosophy of Blackstone with its ante-evolutionary view of society and of an unalterable standard of justice, has gained sway over the minds of our lawyers and judges, with the result of making our administration of justice a national scandal.

Through the efforts of thoughtful jurists like Professors Wigmore, Pound, and others, the American Association of Law Schools at its annual meeting in 1910 officially recognized the necessity of a conscious philosophy of law as a way out of the *impasse* into which we have got by pseudo-intellectualism and the empirical manipulation of cases. The committee appointed by that Association, finding

---

12 See Pound, *Harvard Law Review,* Vol. XXV., pages 166-168.

no English or American philosophy of law, planned to translate a series of important continental works on this subject; and four volumes have already been published. In their general preface the committee begins with the Platonic dictum, "Until either philosophers become kings or kings philosophers states will never succeed in remedying their shortcomings." "And if," continue these lawyers, "he was loath to give forth this view, because as he admitted it might sink him beneath the waters of laughter and ridicule, so today among us it would doubtless resound in folly if we sought to apply it again in our own field of state life, and to assert that philosophers must become lawyers or lawyers philosophers, if our law is ever to be advanced into its perfect workings. And yet there is hope, as there is need among us today, of some such transformation."

"Without some fundamental basis of action, or theory of ends, all legislation and judicial interpretation are reduced to an anarchy of uncertainty. It is like mathematics without fundamental definitions and axioms. Amid such conditions no legal demonstration can be fixed even for a moment. . . . Even the phenomenon of experimental legislation, which is peculiar to Anglo-American countries, cannot successfully ignore the necessity of having social ends" (p.v.).

To cooperate with the American Association of Law Schools in this essential task of philosophy, to examine anew the problem of social ends in relation to law and morals and the life of civilization, would, I believe, be one of the most effective services which our Association can render to our national life as well as to the validity of philosophic study. This will undoubtedly mean our taking up empirical facts which we have regarded as belonging to alien fields. But it is precisely this readiness to take up facts from alien fields that has made the various physical sciences fruitful. Perhaps philosophy is the only profession that has not lately been raising its standard of prerequisite general knowledge. We have been directing our efforts almost exclusively to the refinement of our methods, but it seems to me we need also the introduction of new material. The vitality of philosophy cannot continue if it adheres to the ideal of a monastic or sterile celibacy, but rather

"All the past of Time reveals
A bridal dawn of thunder peals
Wherever Thought hath wedded Fact."

CHAPTER SIX

The Sanctity of Law:
A Critique

T HE HEBREW prophets, the moral teachers of Greece, and other wise men have always preached against idolatry, against setting up the work of human hands as sacred objects of worship, and this applies to the law so far, at least, as it is the work of men. This duty of thoughtful people to examine the law of their land critically and to test whether it does or does not promote human well-being is an especial duty today, when so many are questioning the value of the law or accusing it of being a means of oppression and one of the principal causes of our economic ills. Let us, then, consider the claims of the friends and the foes of our legal system.

From time immemorial the law has been conceived as having divine sanction. According to the Hebrews the law was given by God himself to Moses on Mt. Sinai, according to the Hindus through Manu. And the Greeks likewise surrounded their early laws with divine sanction. The great European tradition which prevailed when our Constitution was adopted was that of natural rights. Nature, according to this view, or the author of nature, laid down certain laws which no creature can disobey without being punished. These principles of natural law are eternal and unchanging and our orthodox view is that the principles of the common law or at least the terms of our Bill of Rights such as due process, and the like, express this type of natural law. The orthodox view is that the judges, especially the judges of the Supreme Court, are there to see that no legislation contravenes these eternal principles.

This conception of the law as emanating from eternal principles has lost repute among scholars and thinkers. Increased study has shown an amazing variation as to what principles are considered just. We say no government has a right to take property from Paul and give it to Peter. Yet that is exactly what every government has always

---

An unpublished paper.

done in the form of taxation, and must continue to do if it is to function at all. We say that every man is entitled to the full produce of his labor. But assuming that in a social world, where things are produced cooperatively, there is some mysterious way of deciding what part of the social product belongs to any one individual, it would still be an open question whether the state has not a right to take away what a man has produced and use it for hospitals, for schools, or nurseries,—that is, to take something away from somebody who has produced it and give it for the support of those who have not produced. In general, the principles of natural law which have been formulated have repeatedly been shown to be meaningless or question-begging. When, therefore, judges, in the name of these principles, decide that certain measures are unjust and therefore unconstitutional, they are substituting their own opinions for the deliberate judgment of our legislatures and it is well to note that the courts by their very constitution do not have as much access to the facts of the case as Congress or the state legislatures. They cannot institute inquiries. They are restricted to briefs and oral arguments of a few hours by two lawyers.

It is a superstition to suppose that the judge's opinions on economic and social questions do not influence his decisions. History belies that assumption. We know perfectly well that when John Marshall was Chief Justice he decided in accordance with the Federalist philosophy and that when Taney succeeded him a different policy prevailed. We know perfectly well that on certain issues which are coming up today certain judges will take an extremely conservative position and certain other judges will take a more liberal position. The assumption that the judge's personal opinion does not count and that every decision is in some mystic sense contained in the Constitution is a childish fiction which is irreconcilable with the actual law or body of decisions.

Not only are many of these decisions arbitrary but some of them are obviously unjust if we take all the facts into account,—for instance, the minimum wage decision in the Adkins case[1] or the decisions in the child labor case[2]. The principle back of the former is the motto of Cain, "Am I my brother's keeper?" These decisions are, according to some of our economists, largely responsible for recurrent depres-

---

[1] Adkins v. Children's Hospital, 261 U. S. 525.
[2] Hammer v. Dagenhart, 247 U. S. 251; Child Labor Tax Case, 259 U. S. 20.

sions. For, it is claimed, they have prevented constructive effort to get us out of the vicious cycle whereby reduction of wages reduces the capacity of our people to buy goods, thus reducing employment, which in turn reduces wages, which in turn reduces still further the whole market. From this vicious cycle it is obvious we cannot be saved except by the community effort to raise the standard of living. There are millions of Americans in the South and the West and in the slums of our richest cities who are living in absolute degradation. This poverty is not due to the stinginess of nature or to our incapacity to produce. Nor is it due to the unwillingness of people to work to support themselves and their children in decent circumstances. Our difficulties are due to the fact that our economic system, fortified by these legal decisions, prevents the farmers' surplus product from reaching those who need it and who in turn are willing to work so that the farmer will have clothing, furniture, and other creature comforts and necessities.

These difficulties are not due to the perverse selfishness of a few individuals. Individual altruism or benevolence will not solve this problem of distribution.

If we wish to deal with the economic problem realistically, we must get rid of fixed *a priori* views. These views come down from a relatively stable society. In such a society certain customs become established and hallowed by use and wont. But they are no longer applicable to a heterogeneous and rapidly changing order. We cannot live by established custom when things are changing or when the ideas of justice of one group conflict with the ideas of justice of another group. We need a better technique for finding ways of adjustment.

The conservatives, those who possess property and other advantages guaranteed by law, naturally insist on the importance of preserving law and order. Few of them, however, care more for the legal system than for their temporary advantage. This shows itself in the open preference for violence. After the First World War the American Legion and other societies of a so-called "patriotic" character came out openly for the suppression of the Socialists, law or no law. When a mob broke into the office of the Socialists' newspaper, *The Call*, destroyed property, and assaulted the men and women who were meeting there, Secretary of the Treasury Glass refused to disown or condemn the action of these overheated patriots. I remember at the time speaking to a justice of the Supreme Court who had had considerable executive experience and who, in reply to my urgent plea that he condemn such action while the courts were still open, said to me, "Too bad that our fellows are doing it." Perhaps the best example of this readiness to throw over the law when it does not promise immediate satisfaction is illustrated by Mr. Owen Wister, who in his Life of Theodore Roosevelt attacks President Wilson because the latter, in conformity to his oath of office, tried to punish a mob in Arizona which had violated the law by assaulting and driving out of town those who wished to exercise the right of free speech. Mr. Wister expressed the opinion of Theodore Roosevelt, who thought it cowardly of a man to protect his rights by calling a policeman instead of assaulting the one who insulted him. It is no wonder, therefore, that those who do not stand to profit immediately by the legal system or rather those whose advantages from our legal system are not so obvious, should be ready to overthrow it or disregard it when it stands in the way of immediate demands.

Disregard of law takes three forms, violence, trickery and revolution. The first presents the problem of crime, the second the problem of preventing clever but unscrupulous men from perverting the law into a means of oppression, and the third the problem of preventing a change of our legal system from involving a bloody civil war in which all the decencies of civilization may be lost.

1. The problem of crime, the tremendous loss which it involves, is one that has been agitating our people considerably in recent years. In no other civilized country is the homicide rate so high. Various commissions have been studying the subject and courses on it are given in our colleges and other schools of learning. But few of us are ready to look at the problem of crime realistically and see its causes.

In the first place, we are confused by pseudo-scientific claims that the criminal is a physical type with a bad heredity or low mentality and we are misled by various efforts to reform the criminal and to enable him to adjust himself to society and become a useful member thereof. But the obvious fact which none can dispute, though few dare face it, is that our reformatories do not reform, that the graduates of our penal institutions drift back into careers of crime and that, at any rate, we are as far from solving the problem of reformation of the criminal as we were at the turn of the century when the new efforts began. And we shall never solve the problem so long as we assume that the problem of adjustment is merely a matter of good will or knowledge, so that whoever is persuaded to turn over a new leaf can do so. All this leaves out of account the fact that crime is a way of making a living,— hazardous to be sure and not in high repute; nevertheless, people who take it up as a business cannot easily find another occupation. Most of our criminals are young people. They see wealth all around them and they have no way of getting the things which they crave. It is a wonder or perhaps a tribute to human inertia that more people do not disregard the law and follow occupations which the law regards as criminal. We shall certainly not reduce crime unless we first remove the temptation which the unequal distribution of wealth brings about. To put water before thirsty people and make a law against their drinking it will breed criminals and will not eliminate crime, no matter how severe the penalty. Hundreds of thousands of people were hanged in England for stealing sums in excess of a few shillings. Yet, that did not solve the problem of crime.

A real understanding of the problem is to be attained only if we all realize how often almost every day each one of us violates the law and that the poor wretches who fill our prisons are merely those who have been caught in the cruder forms of law violation. How many of us violate traffic rules, how many of us are scrupulously careful not to swear off the personal property tax, to declare every article brought from abroad at its true value? It would be, indeed, a very strange spectacle if another Jesus came and asked us that only he who had never committed a crime should cast the first stone at the criminal.

2. The truth is that between the criminal and the non-criminal there is an intermediate realm filled with those who are constantly violating the law but are amply protected by legal technicalities or evasions. I shall not discuss the various forms of racketeering which exist because business men pay for them or find it more economical to pay tribute rather than depend upon the police. The business men of our country readily grow indignant at the corruption of our politicians who are open to bribery and like offenses. But who bribes these corrupt politicians? Who contributes the large funds which the political machines use? Graft in politics is only a drop in the very large bucket of graft in business and if business were done honestly and within the law the politicians could not levy blackmail.

Clearly, in the struggle to have one's will prevail as law, the men of wealth have enormous advantages over all others. They can hire publicity agents, they can organize press bureaus, they can swamp Congressmen and Senators with hundreds and thousands of telegrams. All these are things which require organization and money and are not open to the poor.

The law may pretend that rich and poor are equal before it but in fact that is not true, and if we go to Sing Sing and find that the overwhelming portion of its inhabitants come from poor people, let us not be deluded by the idea that the rich are not there because of their superior moral courage. The fact is that the temptation to crime is mainly for the poor man. The rich do not get arrested for begging in the streets, for sleeping in the subway, for soliciting in the streets, or for the various retail forms of larceny and robbery. The difference is largely due to social-economic status.

3. Normally, people, no matter how oppressed, will follow the government and the legal system. And the whole of history is a record of the patience with which people have suffered tyranny and despotism of the worst sort. At the dawn of history we see great pyramids erected whereby hundreds of thousands of men labored for years to erect monuments to the vanity of certain kings. These monuments, however, are also monuments to the antiquity of human docility. If the skulls of the men who died in the late war were piled up in the form of pyramids they would loom larger than the pyramids of Egypt and they would be a grim reminder of the extent of human docility to government to this day.

This fact of human docility I emphasize because it seems to me the dominating fact in the human attitude to law. It is not wise to ignore it, though it is foolish to ignore the fact that human docility is not infinite and that revolt against oppression is not only possible but often desirable.

What is the cause of this docility and submissiveness? Let us, in the first place, get rid of the notion that government rests on brute force alone. There is no doubt that every government needs some force to maintain order and those utopians who think that by some changes in our economic system men will become reasonable and follow the rules necessary for a common life are egregiously mistaken. Consider, for instance, our traffic rules. Surely, no class of people can deny that they are necessary for the common good. Yet the very people who urge their adoption are ready to violate those rules when they think they can escape punishment. Complete rationality is not as yet a human trait and we all realize in our saner moments that a certain element of compulsion is necessary. The police force and the army thus rest upon the willingness of people to pay taxes for the support of the police and army in order to maintain order and protect the public peace. How many people in New York City, which may be assumed to have its full share of revolutionary ardor, will vote, if the issue is put to them tomorrow, to save money by abolishing the police and the army and all military force. Obviously, only a very small minority. The vast majority want the existence of force.

We may go somewhat deeper and notice that the demand for government rests not only on the fear of disorder but on the positive need for being governed. Most people find deliberation and the necessity of making a choice very painful. It requires thought, which is not to most people an agreeable exercise. And it requires the assumption of responsibility, which most people find vexatious. To find somebody to decide for us and to obey his orders is a relief for which people are willing to pay heavily.

In addition, habit or routine has a value which is essential to life. Governments rest on this need for protecting the routine of life. This desire for routine, corresponding to Newton's first law of inertia, is the fact against which all revolutionary ardor sooner or later dashes itself like the billows of the sea against the sands. Nevertheless, there are limits to human endurance and just as in the Orient despotism is tempered with assassination, so in Western civilization the threat of revolution is always with us. If people care enough about certain things, routine ideologies will not stand permanently in their way.

We are living today at a time when men's tempers are frayed and their patience at low ebb. Men are proposing desperate measures and between revolution to the right and revolution to the left, all the values of civilization, all the gains which science has brought about through the development of the free intellect, are in danger. It is the duty of men of intelligence and good will to see that sheer blindness does not prevail over that bit of light which the experience of the ages has supplied us.

CHAPTER SEVEN

Italian Legal Philosophy

T HE PHILOSOPHY of law has been predominantly and, at times, almost exclusively, an Italian subject. The philosophic ideas at the basis of classical Roman law were, to be sure, Hellenic in origin. But Italian administrative genius was certainly one of the conditions of that continuous development which made Roman law fit to be the law of the world. This administrative genius, as a fine perception of the way to reconcile conflicting interests into a harmonious whole, is perhaps best seen in the greatest of all Italian philosophers, St. Thomas of Aquino, whose formulation of the nature of law is still authoritative for the hundreds of millions who adhere to the Catholic Church.

When, after the death of Hegel, the heroic period of German philosophy began to wane and legal studies throughout Europe became either purely historical or else dominated by narrowly practical considerations, the Italian Universities were the only ones to maintain chairs specifically devoted to the teaching of the philosophy of law. Until the rise of Mussolini, these chairs were maintained despite persistent efforts by ideaphobists and utilitarians to make the law-curriculum more immediately practical.

Thus, notwithstanding the keen revival of interest in the philosophy of law which occurred towards the end of the 19th Century in Germany and France, Italy remained far in the lead as to the number of books in this field. Many of these books would, to be sure, elsewhere be called treatises on jurisprudence or general theory of law. Still, the tradition that views the law in connection with the problems of human nature and the social (if not always cosmic or divine) order is firmly rooted in Italy.

I.

Two factors have served to establish this tradition, to wit, the character of Italian legal studies and the influence of Vico on Italian philosophy.

Published in *Harvard Law Review,* Vol. 59, p. 577 (1946). Reprinted by permission of the publisher.

1. Classical Roman law, with its conception of jurisprudence as "the knowledge of things human and divine" and its precise methodical principles (which made Leibniz compare the Roman jurists to mathematicians) has never completely ceased to be authoritative or an object of study in Italy. For one thing, the law of the Church was too intimately connected with later Roman law. Also, as the Lombards assumed a leading position in Occidental commerce, their leading cities like Pavia developed law schools; and this close connection between Roman, Canon, and (Teutonic) Lombard laws, brought something of the comparative and scientific interest into their study. At any rate, the former Lombard city of Bologna became for centuries the world's center for juristic study and the nursery for training the founders of such studies in France, England, and Germany.

When Gratian compiled and edited the Decretum, Bologna became also the chief seat for the study of Canon law; and though the latter has in fact prevailed throughout the world and has exerted potent influence on the private law and civil procedure of England and other European countries, the study and scientific elaboration of it has been in the main, and at times completely, in Italian hands. Gratian's method of introducing harmony into seemingly discordant canons or authorities, is one of the earliest and most typical expressions of what in philosophy is known as the scholastic method. This method found even greater development in the juristic tradition developed by Bartolus and his followers who sought to harmonize respect for received authorities with the practical needs of the community. The great vogue of the scholastic method in law as in philosophy was not due, as the complacently ignorant have supposed, to the universal stupidity of mankind in those centuries. It was due rather to the fact that this method best served the needs of the times. It enabled the Italian city-states to avail themselves of Saracen learning, to reform procedure (e. g., to introduce the office of public prosecutor), to bring equitable principles into the substance of the commercial and other branches of the law, to invent election by ballot, to discover the principles which form the permanent foundation of what is still the law of private international relations, and to lay the foundations of the science of international public law (in the work of Gentilis and others)—all this, without impairing the respect for tradition which is the principle of order in a fixed-land economy. This is not the place to retell the story

of how, when Roman legions were no more, Italian jurists and mer-
chants as well as Italian clerics, spread civilization. I am merely calling
attention to the fact that the much-abused scholasticism of the Italian
method of studying jurisprudence (*Mos Italicus*) did not prevent the
broad vision which is the essence of philosophy.

Though the Humanist method in jurisprudence, initiated by Alciati,
was primarily animated by the desire to recover the fullness of ancient
life, its vitality and profound sympathy with the individual rights
which the Roman law protected could not but have a reformist effect.
It did in fact break down many medieval restraints and prepared the
way for those great changes in public and private criminal and civil
law which are associated with the age of the Enlightenment. In this
age—a period of political oppression and economic desolation for
Italy—at least two Italian jurists achieved European pre-eminence,
viz., Beccaria and Filangieri. The civilized world was profoundly
stirred by the small but weighty book of Beccaria, *Dei Delitti e delle
Pene,* in which the whole philosophy of the Enlightenment found a
notable humanitarian application. The contemporary French, English,
and other translations of the youthful Filangieri's *Scienze de Legis-
lazioni* show how his generalization of Beccaria's legal humanism
impressed the European mind. This juristic humanism took root in
northern as well as in southern Italy. It can be seen at the end of the
18th and at the beginning of the 19th century in the political writings
of M. Pagano and in those of Romagnosi on criminal and public law.
The struggle for unity in the 19th Century and the consequent task
of combining the laws of the different Italian states and of codifying
the new commercial and penal law all have served to give Italian
legal study a breadth of outlook which makes for philosophy.

2. In Italian philosophy of the 19th and 20th centuries Vico
occupies a position similar to that of Kant in German philosophy.
All schools claim him as their own. There is, however, an important
difference. While Kant began life as a mathematical physicist, and
one of his primary aims was to lay a philosophic basis for Newtonian
physics, Vico was through and through a humanist whose work entirely ignored the great scientific revolution accomplished by Coper-
nicus, Galileo, and Newton. The burning of Bruno, the imprisonment
of Campanella, and the trials of Galileo, had put a quietus on the
bold Italian effort to create a philosophy of nature. Men could not

think freely with the shadow of imprisonment over every unorthodox thought. When, at the beginning of the 18th Century, philosophy timidly began to raise its head again in Italy, it imitated the French Cartesian model—in that faint-hearted way so effectively ridiculed in France by Molière. This could not satisfy a profound and autodidactic spirit such as Vico, who had brooded long on the ancient classics and on the historic speculations of St. Augustine. Where his contemporaries looked for abstract principles, Vico sought historic realities. Instead of the Cartesian 'flair' for starting the world anew, Vico saw the superior force of historic continuity of development.

Thus, altogether out of tune with all that was characteristic of 18th Century thought, Vico was forced back on reflections which contained the seeds of almost everything characteristic of social science two centuries after the publication of his *Scienza Nuova*. Instead of the individual, he took the nation as the unit of social life and development. Social, instead of individual psychology became his Ariadne thread. Hence, instead of viewing social institutions as the result of contract, and religion, law, and poetry as individual inventions, he saw in them the traces of national character in the various stages of development. He thus anticipated the characteristic 19th Century points of view in social psychology, in critical history, in comparative philology, mythology, jurisprudence and science of religion. The one respect in which Vico differed radically from the 19th century point of view was in his cyclical view of the historic evolution of nations, according to which the number of stages of development is strictly limited, so that after completing an historical cycle nations return to an earlier stage. Here, however, Vico, by returning to the more ancient view anticipated the thought of the 20th Century.

One so out of tune with the main current of 18th century thought naturally received little attention except in his own city of Naples. However, with the reaction against the abstract philosophy of the French Revolution and the awakening of Italian national feeling, men began to find in Vico food for thought on the issues which concerned them most. The new intellectual leaders of Italian nationalism, Mario Pagano, Vincenzo Cuoco, and others, found their gospel in his glorification of the Italian mind, to the extent of insisting on its independence even of Greek tutelage.

In the first part of the 19th century French philosophy became flat and had lost its flavor, while German philosophy was not yet well known in Italy. The period of the Risorgimento thus ran the vogue of native schools of philosophy. Gallupi, to be sure, showed the influence of Locke, and Rosmini, that of the Scotch schools of Reid and Stewart, but all schools naturally turned to the national philosophy of Vico. Spiritualists like Gioberti and eclectics like Mamiani found in Vico's conception of the creative power of the mind a form of idealism suitable to the Italian spirit. Likewise, positivists and metaphysical agnostics like Ferrari found Vico's historical method to their taste. Had not the historian Michelet glorified Vico before Europe, and had not Comte acknowledged the latter as one of his forerunners? In any case, men interested in problems such as those of nationality, the relation of church and state, the legal order and the theory of revolutions, found Vico full of suggestions; and this could not but strengthen Italian devotion to the philosophy of law.

Hence, when the wave of historicism engulfed European theory of law, Italy did not completely succumb. It had in Vico all of Savigny's emphasis on historic continuity and yet something more of philosophic perspective.

The various schools of Italian philosophy thus continued to regard the problems of the nature of law as worthy of their major interests. The Rosminian school found European representation in the works of Boistel, Dean of the Law Faculty at the Sorbonne; and the *Philosophy of Right* of Dr. Lioy, a follower of Gioberti, was translated into German, English, and other European languages. Mancini and Mamiani carried into international law the same emphasis on the principle of nationality which Mazzini preached in the field of politics. Count Mamiani's *Il Nuovo Diritto Europeo* (1859) reached the European public in French and in English translations. Actuated by Vico, though in some respects by way of critical reaction, Amari and others initiated studies in comparative jurisprudence, guided by the Viconian belief in a theodicy manifesting itself by the progressive adaptations of laws. Later in time, though actuated in the main by this national tradition, came the works of Carle, works still worthy of the most careful attention. It is well to note in passing, that not only nationalism, but the criticism of nationalism in jurisprudence, has found thoughtful expression in Italy, notably in the work of Brussa, and Fiore. Thus the parallelism between law and language so much relied on by Savigny as well as Vico, found one of its earliest criticisms in Amari, a follower of Vico.

II.

After the triumph of the national cause, the national schools of philosophy began to lose influence. The foreign oppressor and the internal political obstacles having been removed, men began to look to general European philosophy for a wider and more positive program. The prestige of natural science (which despite the great names of Volta, Galvani, and Melloni, had flourished more prosperously in France, Germany and England, since the middle of the 17th century) gave the positivistic philosophy great vogue. The scientific methodology of Comte and the evolutionism of Spencer seemed to offer aid and light on all social and legal problems.

This movement found embodiment in a striking personality Roberto Ardigò. Brought up as a priest, his independent spirit and his patriotic devotion to the national cause led him to leave the church and to become a leader in the movement for scientific enlightenment. He became a professor at Padua and by a series of books impressed Europe as well as his younger countrymen as a solid, useful and enlightened thinker. Living a vigorous life up to the age of 90 he became known as the Patriarch of Padua and his influence on several generations of Italians was profound.

Ardigò conceived of justice as the indication of the healthy or proper functioning of the social organism. Hence sociology, regarded as the science of social welfare, became identical with the philosophy of law. Ardigò's practical idealism was strong enough to make him give full recognition to the power of ideal aspirations in moulding the law. But the rather narrow positivistic view of the nature of science made him and his followers (e.g., A. Levi) distrust as unscientific the strictly ethical point of view in jurisprudence, the point of view which is interested primarily in what the law ought to be. The positivistic school was also somewhat too fatalistic in its conception of the genesis and potency of social ideals.

A somewhat more critical form of juristic positivism was developed by Vanni. Influenced by Maine and the German historical school of jurisprudence, he distrusted all forms of the classical natural-rights philosophy. But besides accepting the German tendency to inquire into the epistemologic basis of juristic knowledge, Vanni was more hospitable to normative jurisprudence and more liberal in believing that social evolution can be influenced by enlightened effort.

Other sociologic jurists like Vaccaro (whose book *Le Basi del Diritto e dello Stato* has been translated into French), have studied the role of law in the struggle for existence. But Vanni has taken the lead in pressing the Malthusian point of view on population. In general the positivistic school has tried to envisage the law as an aid in man's struggle to achieve a greater social order. Just law adapts man to the social order, but a social order that is itself growing. The great contribution, therefore, of this school is in showing the social demands on the law. For a survey of such demands in the realm of private civil law, I know no more useful book than Cosentini's *La Riforma della Legislazione civile.* (The French translation has a preface by Picard in addition to the introduction by Salvioli.)

In the field of criminal law the positivist school of Lombroso, Ferri, Garofalo, *et al.,* has acquired an international reputation not at all agreeable to the prevailing idealistic trend of today. If we ignore, however, the highly questionable deterministic dogmas of this school, we must recognize two of its great achievements; it has shown the moral and intellectual necessity for studying the criminal as a human being and for making punishment something more than blind vengeance irrespective of who is affected and how. Some of the statistical methods which Lombroso first used are clearly defective. But we now see that there can be no enlightened criminal law that is not based on actual study of criminals; and while the idea of hospital treatment for criminals may be of very limited application, the idea of adapting the punishment to the actual individual instead of to the abstract crime, is gaining recognition everywhere.

The positivistic school, true to the Viconian tradition, has been interested in the psychology of law—Micelli, Puglia and others have raised the issues of the psychology of custom, of social pressure in legislation, of the psychology of legal interpretation and of popular obedience. Scientific psychology will have a fruitful task in verifying by experimental and statistical methods the results obtained by these more speculative analytic methods.

Suggestive hints as to the psychology of symbols in modern law have been made by the historian Ferrero.

To the positivistic school also must go the credit for notable contributions to ethnologic jurisprudence, especially the work of Maza-rella. The latter, in the belief that the unity of legal science is to be found in ethnology, has made the most extensive studies of ancient legal systems, such as the Babylonian, and has sought in their analyses the irreducible elements of juristic system. (*Gli Elementi Irredutibili dei Sistemi Giuridici.*) He has also studied the relation of the law to various social types.

It is hard for us today to realize how slowly the German philosophy of Kant and Hegel made its way into Italy. Hegelian idealism came in through translations and expositions by Vera and B. Spaventa. In the literary history of De Sanctis it found its most notable display of power to widen the human vista. In the field of the philosophy of law its most notable representatives have generally been supposed to be Filomusi-Guelfi and Miraglia. The works of Filomusi-Guelfi are certainly idealistic and his *Enciclopedia Giuridica* has been especially influential. His Hegelianism, however, was submerged by the influence of Vico. Miraglia (see his *Filosofia del Diritto*) is so full of Spencer, Vico and other heterogeneous elements, that it is hard to identify him with any special school, except that of general and generous idealism. (His book has been translated in the Modern Legal Philosophy Series as Comparative Legal Philosophy.) Other idealistic writers like Rensi, Petrone, and Barillari have their Hegelian elements in check by Kantian criticism, even though Barillari adheres to the Hegelian conception of absolute knowledge.

It is curious that despite the great interest in Hegelian philosophy aroused by Croce and Gentile—an interest shown by the study and translation into Italian of our own Josiah Royce—Italian jurisprudence can show no genuinely Hegelian work. Possibly the Hegelian dialectic and its frequent violent identification of opposites is too remote from the Italian intellectual tradition and temperament. Yet surely no philosopher ought to be more congenial to the glorification of the state as the supreme authority, than Hegel who characterized the state as God on earth.

If Karl Marx be regarded as an Hegelian—as he should be—we may note that his work found significant development in the writings of Arturo Labriola, one of Croce's teachers. Croce's own economic interpretation and his reduction of the philosophy of law to economics, are in no sense Hegelian, but are actuated by Croce's own views as to the psychologic nature of law, viz., that the law deals with volitions for the attainment of interests. However, Italian jurists and economists like Minghetti have frequently pointed out that the law regulates also human relations in which economic motives do not enter.

In the philosophy of law the Kantian form of idealism is still the more prevalent probably due to the fact that many of the older Italian jurists have studied in Germany or have been influenced by German models. As the chief representatives of this school we may name Petrone and Del Vecchio, the Rector of the University of Rome.

Petrone tries to make clear the fact that the legal order is mental or spiritual reality, and that it must be ruled by transempirical ideals such as the one involved in respect for personality. Del Vecchio has touched on many aspects of the philosophy of law. Here I can only refer to his work as a critic of positivism and as a defender of a genuinely philosophic Jus Naturale. By adhering to the Kantian distinction between the variable experimental content and the rational form, Del Vecchio shows that the historic variability of law in regard to content does not and cannot deny a universal concept applicable to all instances of law and determining whether they are law. But unlike the Hegelians he distinguishes between the logical concept of law and the ideal of what the law ought to be. Natural law is not an additional code of laws but the criterion by which to estimate the value of positive law. Our conception of this criterion may grow in time, but its meaning or validity transcends any one instant of time. In the main this criterion is the Kantian concept of justice—a social order which makes possible the greatest freedom of all individual personalities living together.

Del Vecchio has not only produced a number of writings of his own (deemed worthy of translation in many languages) but he founded and has edited the *Rivista Internazionale di Filosofia del Diritto,* to which the world's leading authorities in this field contribute. He has also refounded the Archivio Giuridico, given over to general studies in jurisprudence.

Besides positivism and the various forms of idealism we must reckon with Neo-scholasticism and more specifically with Neo-Thomism. Since the famous Bull "Aeterni Patris" of Leo XIII, the philosophy of St. Thomas has been officially adopted as a basis of instruction in Church schools, seminaries, etc. This has been a powerful stimulus to the awakening of general interest in the Thomist-Aristotelian tradition. While always claiming a divine sanction for Kings and other duly constituted political authorities, the Church has always insisted that the laws of the state are void when in conflict with natural or divine law. Since the Reformation and the setting up of the modern absolute national monarchies, the Church has had to protest most actively against state absolutism as taught by Bodin and Hobbes.

In the first half of the 19th Century, Rosmini tried to work out a specifically Catholic philosophy of law and the state. Various publications still attest to the vitality of his thought and of the order of charity which he founded. But apart from questions as to his liberalism or concessions to the spirit of the modern age, Rosmini's philosophy was too much his own, and too hostile to the Aristotelian roots of the great medieval doctors, to be a safe basis for an essentially historic church. Hence the more realistic views of men like Ventura and Liberatore on law and on the relation of Church and State have prevailed. Neo-Thomism now has a special organ of its own, the Revista Neo-Scholastico. But even in the universities outside of the Church, men are paying considerable attention to the Thomist conception of law. Recently, for instance, it has been made the basis of a very vigorous and interesting critique of the positivistic, formalistic, and idealistic schools of jurisprudence in a book by Biavaschi (*La Crisi attuale della Filosofia del Diritto.*)

The recent codification of the fundamental law of the Church in the Codex Juris Canonici has led to a good deal of reflection as to the fundamental nature of law and the process of its interpretation. Students of the philosophy of law will find a good deal of it of the utmost importance.

III.

Can we, despite all these diversities, point to some dominant trait of Italian legal philosophy? I think we can find it in the peculiar tenacity with which it has maintained the view that law exists in and for organized society. When the maxims of individualistic *laissez faire* were on the lips of all who wished to be regarded as enlightened, Italian philosophy of law continued to stress communal realities and communal needs. When it was fashionable to speak of legal institutions as results of artificial invention or contract, the first notable criticism came from Vico and Spedalieri. Very early in the 19th Cen-

tury Romagnosi was one of the first to show the necessity of public
control over natural resources such as forests, in order to protect the
welfare of future generations. In this he has been followed by
Mengotti, Messedaglia and others who developed the significance of
the connection between forests and water resources. When increased
productivity was the universal fetish in economics, the ethical tradition of Italian jurisprudence made it refuse to leave the human
worker out of account.

The emphasis on economic conditions as a clue to the understanding
of the nature of law is now associated with Karl Marx and socialism.
Italy, however, can claim that more than twenty years before Adam
Smith published his *Wealth of Nations,* one of her philosophers,
Genovesi, lectured on political economy (in the vernacular) and
showed its significance in relation to ethics and to the broader questions of social policy. Romagnosi, too, was quite explicit in his
emphasis on the economic basis of public law. This question was
somewhat in abeyance when the struggle for national unity was in the
foreground. But the movement now known as the socialization of the
law, the movement to make the law conscious of its obligations to all
classes of society and especially to the weak and the oppressed, found
its leading supporters in Italy in the eighties. (See the works of
Vidale-Pappale, E. Cimbali and others.)

Though Italy was not then an industrial country—certainly not to
the extent of England or Germany—Italian jurists were among the
first to urge that modern codes and the individualism of Roman law
failed to do full justice to the interests of the laboring classes. They
were among the first to elaborate the theory that as work accidents
are an inevitable part of the industrial risk altogether apart from the
question of fault, their cost should be borne by the industry rather
than by the unfortunate victim and his dependants. (Fusinato, *Gli
Infortuni del Lavoro.*)

However, the ethical limitations of the theory of social insurance
were well worked out by Zammarano who showed that insurance
could not remove unjust inequalities.

It is not a pure accident that when an American, David Lubin, was
looking for some country to sponsor the International Institute of
Agriculture, Italy was the one to welcome his beneficent idea. It had
for a long time given unusual attention to the demands which agri-

culture can justly make on the law. In this connection it is interesting to note that the most extreme Italian proponent of the class struggle as a clue to legal and other history, A. Loria, takes the land system as the basis of his speculations rather than the system of industrial production as do the Marxians.

Italian jurists and economists, among them the famous P. Rossi, have elaborated a national defense for what to American individualists must seem a most uneconomic institution, viz., the system of the reserve which restricts the power of testamentary disposition so that a certain portion must go to the heirs. This again illustrates the concern of Italian philosophy of law with the importance of family continuity so neglected by extreme individualism.

The tendency of Italian jurists to make the technical, social, and economic nature of transactions the decisive consideration in moulding the law (as contrasted with the predominantly exegetical and historical methods in vogue elsewhere) is perhaps best seen in the realm of commercial law. Vivanti, the editor of the *Rivista Di Diritto Commerciale,* and the author of a great treatise on the subject which has received preeminent European recognition, has blazed new paths by his fresh analysis of the nature of credit instruments, business partnerships, agency, and similar legal ideas.

Those interested in the philosophy of public law will find in the work of Mosca and Pareto the most serious realistic analysis of the basis of general government in the light of the general social division of labor. These writers have not allowed the prevailing fictions of representative government to blind them to the real difference of interests between the group that governs and those that obey. Though various points in their theory are highly debatable they have undoubtedly uncovered one of the real difficulties in the theory of democracy. Their work has been applied by R. Michels to explain in a most illuminating way the internal structure and functioning of the German Social Democratic Party. No student of the theory of general government can afford to ignore this book, *The Sociology of Political Parties.*

Finally, Italian philosophy of law has shown a sense of its own responsibility in the making of the law. That the interpretation of the law is not a merely linguistic or logical process but involves also the weighing of social considerations, was pointed out by Italian jurists Diena and Scialoja long before Gény made this one of the central issues of modern legal theory. Though Italy has not produced any one work comparable to Gény's *Méthodes,* the active role that judge and jurist play in the making of the law was noted by the national juridical congress at Palermo in 1903, some time before the issue received general recognition elsewhere. The philosophy of law in Italy has had a broad base in the general interests of jurists and philosophers.

CHAPTER EIGHT

Should Legal Thought
Abandon Clear Distinctions?

THE EXACT meaning of the title of Lon L. Fuller's book, *The Law in Quest of Itself*, and its relevance to the contents of the book are not quite clear to me; but two distinguishable themes seem to me fused in the author's mind. Professor Fuller's major objective, I take it, is to show the inadequacy of any account of the law which isolates it entirely from the social *mores* and prevailing sentiments of right and wrong. On this theme Professor Fuller makes some decidedly worth-while and telling points. It should be added, however, that some (but certainly not all) of those he attacks as "realists" and "positivists" have been urging the same thing in somewhat different terms. Though I, for example, am by implication put in the category of the positivists, I have been for more than a quarter of a century advocating an avowedly normative jurisprudence, as the application of judgments of value or social ethics to legal institutions; and I have not been afraid to call it a return to natural law. (See e. g., "Jus Naturale Redivivum" in the *Philosophical Review*, 1915, and "The Process of Judicial Legislation" in *The American Law Review*, 1914.)

But while I regard this integrative task as necessary, it seems to me fatal to try to meet it by disregarding clear distinctions and confusing the theory of law with vague or questionable moral ideas and sentiments. For this reason, I think it worth-while to pass over the merits of Professor Fuller's book in regard to what he may deem his major argument and devote this review to a criticism of his subsidiary theme, viz., his opposition to "that direction of legal thought which insists on drawing a sharp distinction between the law that *is* and the law that *ought to be*" (p. 5). When I first read this passage I could not believe that a professor of law of Fuller's eminence would object to such a necessary and obviously clear distinction which he himself

---

A review of *The Law in Quest of Itself* by L. L. Fuller, in *Illinois Law Review*, Vol. 36, p. 239 (1941). Reprinted by permission of the publisher.

frequently makes and must make. And so I supposed that the word *distinction* was a linguistic slip, and that he meant only to protest against the *separation* of law from all its social and ethical sources and implications. But further reading of this book (e.g., pp. 10, 85, 91, 108, 112) showed unmistakably that Professor Fuller is definitely hostile to this clear distinction and really prefers to "tolerate a confusion" (p. 5) and to "obscure the boundary between law and morality and to import into the law the looser and freer ways characteristic of ethical thinking" (p. 130). In view of the devastating effects of loose thinking on morals to which the history of mankind amply testifies, it is well to be on guard against loose thinking as a proposed salvation for jurisprudence.

The failure to discriminate clearly between *distinguishing* and *separating* is one of the great obstacles to the advancement of real understanding. To separate two phases of a subject is to ignore their interconnections, while to distinguish the two is to clarify them and their function in the totality which includes them. The baffling character of life's practical problems consists largely in the difficulty of finding the factors in any given situation that are relevant to our purpose and distinguishing them clearly from what is irrelevant. If we cannot make the necessary distinctions we are swamped by irrelevancies. The elimination of irrelevancies may over a long period be brought about by a process analogous to natural selection, but in the exact sciences it is more readily effected by mathematical or logical analysis. In the inorganic field such analysis is aided by the process of actual physical separation of the various elements of the object before us. We often find how a mechanism works or how to deal with a physical object by resolving it into its parts and putting them together again. But this is not so frequently possible with organisms that die in the process of dissection, and much less is it possible in regard to human societies that do not allow themselves to be experimented upon like fruit flies or guinea pigs. Here then we have to depend on mental analysis, on abstracting or picking out for our attention the various individual threads and tracing the course of each before we can understand their connection in the complicated tangle before us. To refuse, therefore, to make any sharp distinction is to shut the gates to any effective intellectual inquiry; while to stop with an abstract distinction and to fail to realize the connection of the things distinguished (which I take to be the basic vice of false separation) is to fail to complete the process of understanding. In trying to avoid the lesser error, Professor Fuller manages, like so many others, to fall into the greater one. There is no possible warrant for his rejecting the sharp distinctions between what is and what ought to be the law, "as a starting point" (p. 7) applicable "to the raw data which experience offers us" (p. 10).

The fact that certain practices exist, often (although fortunately not always) leads us to believe that they are right or ought to be maintained, and the belief that a certain law, custom, or existing state of affairs ought not to be, sometimes leads to its modification or abolition. But while what exists and what ought to exist are thus connected, they are quite distinct and in no way identical. Indeed, like husband and wife, father and child, or the poles of a magnet, they could not be connected if they were not distinct. Pope's dictum, "whatever is, is right," logically denies the existence of wrong; and no one who has suffered injustice in this world consistently believes in this silly and infamous dictum. The bitter cry of men and women against outrageous laws or practices (which some fanatics have regarded as moral) fills the history of all peoples throughout the ages. Nor does anyone really believe that the popular feeling that a given law ought to be abolished or enacted is identical with its actual legal repeal or enactment. Surely there are legislative enactments (within our Constitution) that Professor Fuller would admit to be so unjust that they ought not to be the law, and yet he would not advise any student to disregard their legal effects.

Logically the distinction between judgments of what exists and of what ought to be is so fundamental that their confusion makes rational argument impossible. If there is anything clear in logic, it is that if our premises are about A it is a non-sequitur to draw a conclusion about B. Hence, from the mere fact that a certain law or state of affairs exists, we cannot draw a logical conclusion as to whether it ought or ought not to continue to exist. We can do so only if we also have an assumption or premise as to whether a change ought to be made. This is so elementary that I supposed no one would question it in this form. Yet Dr. Brecht in a recent number of the *Harvard Law Review* has tried to escape this obvious truth by saying that while it is undeniable in formal or deductive logic, it is different in inductive logic. Such a claim, however, makes inductive logic meaningless or a *contradictio in adjecto*. Induction is a process of generalization, reasoning from the characteristic of a number of samples or instances to the nature of a whole class to which they belong. Such generalizations are guesses which turn out to be true if the class of which we have samples is homogeneous in regard to the given characteristic. There can be no induction from the property of anything to that which is generically different from it.

In our daily experience, ethical judgments are unavoidable and apt to be taken for granted so that it is not necessary to state them explicitly. Thus, in giving the reason why certain practices should be avoided we often say that they are unnatural or abnormal, and so we speak as if a rule as to what we ought to do can be derived from premises as to what merely exists. A mother, for instance, tells her daughter, "Don't wear that hat. Nobody wears it this season," to which the daughter can reply, "But I am wearing it." Obviously the force of the mother's plea is based on the assumption that we *ought* not to wear a hat that is not in fashion, i.e., that a majority of the "best" people do not wear. But if the daughter cares not for fashion, or prefers to wear a hat which like a fitting frame enhances the beauty of her head and face, the mother's argument breaks down. She might come back with the retort, "People will think you queer." To which the daughter might well reply, "I don't care," or "I prefer that they notice me." This homely example illustrates the fundamental fallacy common to many positivists and *some* adherents of natural law who try to deduce what the law ought to be from propositions that assert only what exists. The medieval forms of natural law are relatively free from this fallacy. Natural law was derived from a command by God. It could be obeyed out of love of Him or fear of His punishments; but man's nature was generally recognized as capable of choosing the evil, even if that involved suffering the consequences. If doing the right were determined by man's nature, the world would be quite different from what it is. Modern jurists do not like to invoke God's commandments as a basis for the discrimination between good and evil. They think they can get the two rabbits "ought to be" and "ought not to be" out of a hat which contains only judgments as to what exists. This is not only logically indefensible, but practically pernicious, for it evades the important task of questioning or critically examining our moral premises, a procedure which distinguishes science, in which all can participate, from the blind dogmatism that divides us into sects. This free scientific criticism of basic principles is essential to liberal civilization. Without it we plunge into passionate but blind conflicts.

Let us now look at Professor Fuller's attempt to prove the impossibility of a sharp distinction between what is and what ought to be the law. Its essence[1] consists in the statements that "the bulk of human relations find their regulation outside the field of positive law *however that field is defined*," (p. 111, italics mine) and "in this field of autonomous order which surrounds the positive law there can be no sharp division between the rule that is and the rule that ought to be." (p. 112). To this amazing argument three obvious observations are pertinent. (1) To those who define law as co-extensive only with what Professor Fuller refers to as positive law, the surrounding "autonomous" field cannot be law at all; and it is pointless to urge that in the void where there is no law there can be no distinction between one kind and another. (2) If we define law to include the customary rules of the "autonomous" field, the distinction between those rules that ought and those that ought not to prevail is still applicable, unless one adopts the infamous doctrine of Pope and willfully denies that there are customs and beliefs as to morals that are more honored in the breach than in the observance. (3) Of greater juristic concern it is to realize the superficiality of the currently fashionable denial that the law regulates the bulk of human relations. This facile denial is due to a failure to discriminate between the expression of specific provisions and the effect of the whole body of law. It is true that we now have no legal provision as to what a testator should wear or whether he shall sign his will with a fountain pen (though popular "natural" law regards signing with a pencil as invalid). We do not even have any prescription that anyone must make a will at all. Under all legal

---

[1] I have restricted myself to Professor Fuller's legal argument. But it ought to be added that he also labors under the fallacious argument that a distinction between the *is* and the *ought* is impossible because the world of fact is a "moving" one (p. 64). This involves a confusion between considerations of existence and judgments of value. The natural world may be moving in a direction conformable or not to our moral ideas of what ought to prevail. The judgment that the *is* and the *ought* are inseparably mixed is true only for those who cannot or do not want to take the trouble of unmixing them in their mind's eye.

systems men have certain choices. But these choices are effective only when adequately protected. Our freedom to travel does not amount to much where there is no police protection or no traffic rules. It is the whole body of governmental or non-autonomous law including criminal, police, and property law, which makes it possible for a man to have any real estate, rents, stocks and bonds, patents or franchises, which he can dispose of. Modern property exists only in the modern state.

The common argument that in most cases we do what we deem right without thinking of the law ignores the fact that the prevailing views as to what is the right thing to do are largely conditioned by our law. And this is true not only in states where legislation originates to some extent in popular demand, but also in non-democratic states. The tax, rent, or game laws of the Norman usurpers and conquerors of England and Ireland, became in a relatively short time the felt moral obligations of a large part of the conquered people. Fear of the consequences of disobeying the law soon transforms itself into general respect for it and consequent disapproval of those who run afoul of it. [I use the word "general" because resentment against unjust laws does not completely disappear in any limited period.]

Indeed after minimizing the importance of positive law (cf. p. 15) and of legislation, Professor Fuller himself comes in the end to recognize the fact that legal rules actually shape our morality (pp. 135-137). He hastens to add that this is peculiarly true of those rules that are judge-made. But his actual illustration, that of traffic regulation, is definitely the result of legislative rather than judge-made law.

In this connection we must also guard against the error of ignoring the tremendous diversity of moral attitudes and standards in modern life. In relatively simple and homogeneous societies living under fairly constant conditions, the prevailing moral feelings may, without much visible outer machinery, regulate conduct sufficiently to secure the necessary minimum of public safety or security. In modern cosmopolitan communities, living under rapidly changing conditions, this is not feasible. A certain amount of diversity as to aesthetic and moral valuation is not only tolerable but even desirable as laying a basis for progress. But legislation or positive law-making is necessary to prevent such diversity from breaking up communal life or making our transactions too insecure.

Historical learning, the outer ritual of scientific or philosophic thought, and imposing footnote references to other writers, are not satisfactory substitutes for clear ideas or insight into contemporary legal problems. With pedants they constitute so much ballast for empty ships. But anyone who wishes an integrated view of the law as part of the whole social process cannot ignore history, social science, and philosophy. And it is obviously of the utmost importance that when ideas from neighboring fields are introduced into jurisprudence, they should rest on the soundest scholarship.

Professor Fuller deems resort to history necessary for understanding the temper of an age. But if the law at any given time is "an accidental configuration without lasting importance" (p. 15), what value can legal history have? His actual excursions into the history of positive and natural law are not very fortunate. He attributes to Hobbes the invention of the doctrine of law as the will of the sovereign. This not only ignores Bodin and others, but misses a good deal of the motive of natural law which was directed against the later Roman view, embodied in the Justinian Code, that law is whatever pleases the prince. Not only medieval but 16th century writers as diverse as Buchanan and the Jesuits used natural law to oppose the power or divine rights of the temporal sovereign. A realization of this as well as of the course of the natural-law doctrine in America (in the form of restraints on legislative power "implied" in "the principles of free or republican government" or "due process") would have prevented Mr. Fuller from confidently asserting that the theory of natural rights of the individual is not an essential part of natural law (p. 100). As a matter of fact, Mr. Fuller's own conception of natural law does not involve a belief in individual natural rights. He fears "the neat hierarchic patterns—in which every man becomes officer to another" (p. 115). But he cannot ignore that many changes have to be brought about by legislative and administrative decree. Obviously, what we need is some reasonable distinction between those realms in which legislation is necessary and those affairs which may better be left to the diverse moral feelings in modern heterogeneous communities. Towards such a solution no system of natural law which is hostile to distinctions between what is and what *ought to be* can possibly contribute. Mr. Fuller's counsel of willful blindness will not help us avoid being wrecked on either the Scylla of totalitarianism or the Charybdis of anarchy. Personally, I do not see how his "subjective relativism" can be distinguished from moral anarchy.

Incidentally, Mr. Fuller is neither accurate nor quite fair when he maintains both that "positivism has dominated American legal thought for nearly a century" (p. 161) and that Holmes is largely responsible for it (p. 117). Natural law as "the failure to distinguish between law and morals," has certainly prevailed in American legal thought, as can be seen in decisions from early colonial times to quite recent days. And Holmes' effort to remove that confusion is a relatively recent attempt. Nor is it fair to ignore Holmes' equally emphatic insistence (for at least fifty years of his life) that the law does contain judgments as to social values which should be carefully studied, and that when courts set aside legislative enactments on the alleged ground of violation of individual rights (supposed to be guaranteed by the Constitution), they are really taking sides on debatable issues as to economic facts without adequate study of the latter. That is the rationale of his significant dissenting opinions and of such essays as *The Path of the Law.*

One who denies a sharp distinction between the law that is and the law that ought to be, obviously cannot, even if he professes to believe in natural law, draw a clear distinction between good and bad laws. Something like this leads Professor Fuller to deny (pp. 92-95) the obvious truth of Justice Holmes' statement that a bad man can use the law for his own evil purposes, a denial that seems to me a veritable *reductio ad absurdum* of our author's position. The appeal to popular loose use of words cannot wipe out the distinction between the term "steam engine" and "good steam engine" (p. 11), or between "a story" and "a good story" (pp. 8-9). The former includes the bad variety which the latter excludes.

Many of Professor Fuller's criticisms of those he calls positivists, e.g., Holmes and Gray, decidedly lack substance. Thus the fact that there is an appeal to the Supreme Court, (p. 50) is no real objection to Gray's realism. Gray asserts not that every judge makes the law, but only that the law is made by the court that finally decides the case. Nor can I see that there is any substantial difference between Gray's "rules laid down," and Holmes' "those acted on," by the court. Both knew that the decision and not the dicta make the law in this case. On the other hand, I see no warrant for Professor Fuller's statement (in arguing against Austin) that judges "habitually talk as if they were principals" rather than agents (p. 24). The fact seems clearly to the contrary. They habitually *talk* as if they had nothing to do but to obey the will of the legislature or of the people in constitutional convention.

The meaning that words acquire in common usage becomes generally habitual and Humpty Dumpty's notion that we can by the fiat of arbitrary definition make any word denote anything we please, is far more vain than most New Year's resolutions to change our habits, since it is hard for any writer or speaker to change also the habits of his readers or hearers. And Professor Fuller's strange definition of positivism and natural law not only does violence to the historic meaning of these terms, but in the end confuses his argument since he cannot avoid inconsistently reverting to the commonly accepted usage. No issue is really clarified by defining positivism so as to exclude Comte, Durkheim, and Duguit, and to include all the great moral teachers and reformers who sharply condemned the existing law because it did not conform to the ideal of what ought to be. It is certainly not true that all writers on natural law have confused the actual and the desirable, though undoubtedly some have done so just like many of those whom Professor Fuller calls positivists. The motives for this confusion are to be sure somewhat different in the two cases. The positivists are actuated by a false conception of scientific method which makes a normative ethics impossible; while natural-law theorists who try to derive what ought to be from existing nature are generally afraid to recognize that all evil and viciousness also have their roots in human nature. In the end, however, the confusionists in both groups dodge the task of making explicit their actual fundamental ethical assumptions.

Professor Fuller criticizes positivism as a formalist theory which altogether disregards the content of the law. But we may search in vain to find in this book any definite indication of either what the content of the law is or what it should be. The "looser and freer ways of thinking" that our genial author chooses to identify with natural law cannot really determine what course is best for lawyers or anyone else. That can be done only on the basis of clear and definite ideas.

The general impression which this book leaves is that of legal as well as moral "stand-patism"[2]; so that if it fairly represented the point of view of natural law it would justify Kelsen's characterization of the latter as essentially static. Certainly Professor Fuller shows little resentment against the outrageous injustices of the law or much sympathy for legal reform. Instead, he displays the old-fashioned law professor's prejudice against legislation. He tries to dispose of the serious and weighty objections to reform through the admittedly slow process of judicial adjudication by saying he is aware of them. This, I submit, in no way minimizes their force. Particularly is this true of the objection that courts (protected by the fiction that they only "declare" the law) persistently refuse to make the urgently needed changes, so that legislation is necessary to make the law at all tolerable. It is significant to note that in the list of objections to reform by the judicial process (p. 133), Professor Fuller omits the most important one; namely, that in the contentious procedure of the common law where the judge is only an umpire, there is no provision for the court instituting any adequate inquiry to become fully acquainted with the social implications of the issues involved in the case. The importance of finding the facts before determining what the law should be does not solicit much of Professor Fuller's attention. But it has appealed to the mass of American people who despite a traditional respect for our courts, amounting at times to idolatry, have instituted commissions like the one on interstate commerce, which can make investigation before deciding what ought to be done—Dean Pound's fulminations against commissions and executive justice to the contrary notwithstanding. The reason that Professor Fuller gives to justify his preference for reform by the judicial process is "that its decrees pass over readily into what I have called the realm of autonomous order. The common law imperceptibly becomes a part of men's common beliefs, and exercises a frictionless control over their activities which derives its sanction not from its source but from a conviction of its essential rightness" (p. 134).

Now I submit that this is a mythology contrary to historic fact. The

---

2 The charge of moral stand-patism is valid against one who restricts morality to those rules which actually do influence men's conduct and thus excludes those rules which ought to, but unfortunately do not, prevail; and Professor Fuller does precisely this. Indeed, he goes so far as to say: "This whole 'extra-legal' body of moral precepts is to a large extent a creature compounded of paper and ink and philosophic imaginations" (p. 136).

persistent demand for legislation would not exist if people venerated "the common law" as much as some law professors do.

In his anxiety for practical results, Professor Fuller seems to lean toward the pragmatic conception of truth. But he definitely fails to appreciate the instrumental value of ideal or limiting concepts such as the postulate of law as a logical system. (How can we consistently hold to the notion that there is a common law in the United States, as Professor Fuller does, if we reject the concept of law as a system?) It is, of course, foolish to regard the latter as a *description* of what the law actually is at any given time. But the notion that all significant or scientific concepts are copies of existing things is the very vice of historic positivism which Professor Fuller and others would have avoided if they had recognized the function of those regulative ideas that point out what may be an ever receding goal but definitely indicate the direction of progress. It is missing the point to argue as if the social contract of Hobbes and other writers on natural law was intended as a description of a past historic event. Careful reading shows that it was used to indicate a logical-analytic scheme for dealing with the ever recurring fact of obedience to law, the fact that men accept and obey restraints laid down by the legal state which are not obeyed in a "state of nature," i.e., unrestrained by law. It is this same positivist myopia which makes Professor Fuller oppose sharp distinctions where nature fails to show it to raw experience. But the sharp distinction between day and night is justified both theoretically and practically even though there be a large twilight zone between them. And the fact that the *ought* and the *is* are mixed in our dark view (p. 64) is no reason against unmixing them in order to clarify things and remove some of the darkness. Difficulties should serve as challenges rather than as prohibitions to the use of intelligence.

Despite Professor Fuller's professed rejection of mysticism from jurisprudence (p. 78) and his frequent invocation of reason (as if none of those he calls positivists believed in it), it is difficult to see how he can deny a definite strain of irrationalism, if not obscurantism, in his distrust of clear ideas and of factual scientific inquiry generally. Though he agrees with the realists that in discussing recent legal decisions extra-legal factors must be taken into account, he does not like the idea of making these factors the objects of the most careful and accurate inquiry, but leans rather to "oracular powers" and the methods of the priest (pp. 127-128). He seems to argue that because a statistical study as to the number of trains that are late is inadequate to determine what is to be done about it (p. 118) such studies can therefore be dispensed with—a popular failure to discriminate between necessary and sufficient conditions. But no one really doubts that diagnosis is necessary for therapeutics, even though it is by itself insufficient.

Professor Fuller makes a remarkably naive objection to the requirement that the writer on law should state clearly whether he is giving his own opinion or stating what the law is as determined by legislatures and courts (pp. 138-140). He fears this might lead some to refuse to write at all! We may not join those who would rejoice at such an outcome, but there is certainly no merit in the argument that such a requirement hinders creative work. On the contrary, it is the condition for it. It is now a general requirement of a scientific memoir that it clearly state what had been done by others and what the author has himself contributed.

It is preposterous to argue that the rigid requirements of the scientific method put any prohibitions against intelligent discussion of the vague and shifting forces which ultimately shape man's living. Science has no power to deny the right of men and women to talk as intelligently or as loosely as they please about anything at all. It only insists on intellectual honesty which forbids us to claim knowledge or the truth of our conclusions when the evidence is inadequate.

Linked to the distrust of science is a distrust of democracy. Professor Fuller fears a democracy based on skepticism. Now it is true that both democracy and scientific procedure involve a skepticism, not as to the existence of justice or the use of reason, but rather as to whether any mortal has a privileged source of truth or knowledge not open to ordinary humanity by the process of verification. The skeptical challenge to all who claim moral or other truth to produce evidence of their claims is the indispensable condition for free and rationally organized society. Without the freedom of the mind to question all authorities, life ceases to be human and becomes slavish and brutish.

This review is perhaps unnecessarily severe on a book whose main aim is to attack some superstitions which pass among some as new discoveries in the science of law; but by deliberately adopting the

Mephistophelian advice to the callow student to despise theory (or the logical clarity of science) in favor of a dim twilight called life (p. 118), Professor Fuller's fight is waged on a "darkling plain where ignorant armies clash at night." Obscurantism does not advance the cause of the good life.

The unfortunate separation of law from ethics, economics, and general philosophy was brought about by the confusion into which the older doctrines of natural law had fallen. We cannot improve things by trying to revive the old errors and confusions. Any proper integration of the different social sciences into an adequate study of law must be based on a clear logical analysis of their different elements. Only when the latter are clearly distinguished and carefully studied can they be intelligently synthesized to meet the needs of wise practice as well as of understanding. A sound doctrine of just or "natural" law thus requires sharper and sounder weapons than this book offers us.

CHAPTER NINE

Law and the Lawyers

T HE MEDIEVAL separation between the arts and sciences taught in the Universities and the common law learnt in the Inns of Court or by being apprenticed to a practicing lawyer, is now being partly overcome by the recent expansion of the American University which makes it seek to integrate the law school into the general scope of its studies. Hence law teaching is no longer a matter of experienced practitioners taking time off to initiate others into the tricks of the trade but is entrusted to those who, like other university professors, are supposed to be engaged in scholarly research to advance our knowledge in their special branch of learning—and such knowledge naturally involves acquaintance with related fields. This tendency—if we cannot as yet call it an achievement—is re-enforced by the fact that with the improved education of bar and bench, there comes the realization that courts can no longer decide the complicated issues of modern life by taking judicial notice of common or traditional information, but must rely to an increasing extent on the aid of expert knowledge in all sorts of fields. There are of course still those who maintain that law is law and has nothing to do with economic, psychologic, or sociologic or other theories. But this view, though still powerfully entrenched in the popular and traditional misconception as to what the courts do when they decide constitutional issues, is so obviously contrary to fact, that we may ignore it when addressing those who have any knowledge of legal history. In general, advanced legal study in America has become so hospitable to all sorts of suggestion from allied and even foreign fields, that English lawyers are somewhat puzzled by what they regard as rather wide departure in our law journals from strictly legal issues.

No friend of enlightenment or of a better administration of justice can wish this to be otherwise. Nevertheless it is well for students of the law to remember that there is at least one thing that law and science have in common and that is a willingness to look at both sides of every

A review of *Law and the Lawyers* by Edward S. Robinson in *Cornell Law Quarterly*, Vol. 22, p. 171 (1936). Reprinted by permission of the publisher.

question and to demand evidence or proof before admitting any proposition. Proposed contributions of psychology, as of philosophy, sociology and economics to the law, should therefore be relentlessly cross-examined before they are admitted as justified in truth. And as Professor Robinson's main contention is the need of more natural science in the law he should be glad if his suggestions receive from lawyers some of that critical caution which is the first requisite of scientific method.

Indeed, in view of the diversity of psychologic schools, to which Professor Robinson calls our attention,—how behaviorists contradict psychoanalysts, and psychiatric experts can generally be found on both sides of any case—we may well suspect that psychologists are made of the same human clay as judges, lawyers and the rest of us, and that not only are they fallible, but that the love and knowledge of the truth is only one of the factors which determines what they say, and that other honorable motives, anterior and more deeply rooted in our nature, such as the desire to lead in or contribute to the improvement of the world, our professional pride and a reliance on the accepted opinions of our group, also play their role.

Now it would not be difficult for an unfriendly critic, provoked by a certain high-and-mighty censoriousness in the book before us, to contrast it with a legal work such as Holmes' *Common Law* and show how much more scientific is the latter in dealing with verifiable knowledge or giving cogent evidence for one's conclusions. He could also point out that it is the psychologist, more than the jurist, who is guilty of vague rhetorical analogies between natural science and social studies—analogies which do not come to grips with actual facts in either field. Such a critic might also point to Professor Robinson's unacquaintance with the mathematical element in modern physical science, as shown in the reference to "irrational" numbers as fictions. This would be all the more easy because, instead of patiently building up a body of empirical evidence for his various contentions, our author states them rather dogmatically as dialectic consequences of traditional but uncritical naturalism, and gives us programs based on that vague faith rather than positive scientific achievements to strengthen it. But such ungracious criticism is a profitless and thankless task. In view of the desperate need in our legal system for more truth or real factual knowledge and less fiction, we should, it seems to me, be as sympathetic as possible with the main point of Professor Robinson's exhortation, to work in that direction even when we are unconvinced by his specific arguments. The sores in our legal system are many and grievous—all the more grievous because many of them have been repeatedly pointed out at least as far back as Bentham. But if they are to be cured by the introduction of more science, we must make certain of the genuineness of the science.

A basic argument which is frequently heard today and which runs through this book, though not always made expilicit, may be put as follows: The law deals with human affairs and human nature. Psychology is the natural science of human nature or conduct. And since all the progress in engineering and medicine has resulted from relying on natural science, it follows that the study of law can be nothing but a branch of psychology, and that the acceptance of this view ought to and will renovate the law.

Though this argument seems plausible, it involves a number of serious misapprehensions. What is natural science? If we view it as designating such studies as physics, chemistry, biology, psychophysics or physiologic psychology, then, indispensable as such knowledge is for jurisprudence, it surely cannot constitute the whole of the latter. If, however, we regard natural science as knowledge which can be verified, or shown to rest on adequate factual evidence, then we must take the position indicated before, viz., that the legal writings of a man like Holmes or Maitland are more scientific than those of psychologists who leave the elementary truths that laboratory experiments have so far yielded and dogmatize about complex regions of human affairs. We certainly cannot, by calling psychology a natural science, deny that a great deal of what is published under its name today is highly speculative and the object of great difference of opinion. The one experimental or statistical study referred to in this book—rather remote in its bearings on the law—is certainly capable of other interpretations than the one given by Professor Robinson. And surely he cannot expect all of us to accept on the authority of the natural science of psychology his rather than Senator Norris' opinion as to the "liberalism" of Mr. Justice Hughes. Nor has psychology as yet proved that judges are free from that class bias to which all other human beings are subject. I venture to think that few acquainted with the literature on the subject will adopt Professor Robinson's opinion on the law of liability, for it fails to take into account many factors of the situation such as the objective need to distribute losses. His statements that crime should be treated like a disease by clinical methods indicate human hopefulness, but there is little support for them in the statistics of reformatories and cases of probation.[1] The confident advice that we should eliminate praise and blame does not, and in the nature of the case cannot, have any empirical evidence for it of the kind that would be regarded as weighty in any natural science.

With some of Professor Robinson's opinions I heartily agree and I hope that time will prove them true; but I should not claim that they are demonstrated by the science of psychology. Dogmatism in the name of science is no better than dogmatism in the name of theology. And I am glad to note that Professor Robinson at times recognizes this, and concludes his book with a quotation from William James to the effect that the value of science is not merely in giving us solutions to special problems (which is surely a good thing as far as it goes), but in opening up our minds to new vistas, of hitherto unknown possibilities. Such wider vision is the essence of liberalism which both law and psychology equally need.

This brings us to the necessity of avoiding a confusion, peculiar to practical Americans, namely the failure to discriminate between science and its practical applications. Engineers and physicians do well to apply as much of science as they can find available for their purpose. But there is an unmistakable difference between the science of physics and engineering, between physiology and pathology and the art of healing. The two should not be confused even if sometimes exercised by the same person.

If we keep this rather obvious distinction in mind we shall not so easily forget, as do Professor Robinson and others, that technology or practice must always to some extent precede science. Men, as a historic fact, knew how to build bridges, various machines, and many other things before modern science came on the scene. We learn to walk before we learn the principles of mechanics, and we learn to talk

---

[1] Professor Robinson assumes that psychiatry is a natural science and that it knows how to cure people. But he does not ask when is a man cured. Reflection might show that, the moment we leave purely physical considerations, the usual criterion employed is the ability to behave in accordance with the social standards of our community, and that is largely a moral standard. The only other test actually used is the patient's own feeling that he is cured and that of course is affected by all sorts of faiths that do not rest on natural science.

our particular language before we acquire an understanding of pho-
netics and philology. Politics assuredly involves a knowledge of
human nature; but from this it does not follow that Messrs. Hitler,
Mussolini, Stalin or any of our successful political bosses could have
learned much to their purpose from our teachers of psychology. I do
not mean that such men can write better books on psychology than
our professors on that subject, but assuredly the latter are not yet in
a position to instruct everyone how to conduct his practical affairs;
and this applies to the law as to other fields. If psychology is based
on human experience, the psychologist must learn, if he can from those
who are in most intimate intellectual contact with that experience.

This observation is not in any way an argument against the cultivation of the science of psychology. Nor does it at all deny that it
may, when sufficiently developed, be an aid to illumine and improve
legal practices. But scientific usefulness or applicability is secondary
to and dependent on scientific integrity. And that means a rigorous
limitations of pretensions. After all science is not what our industrial-
ists and Puritan moralists foolishly suppose it to be, namely, a mere
means for more practical achievements. Some of the most developed
branches of mathematics, and physical as well as biologic science have
never as yet found any practical application and may never do so.
Indeed, experimental physicists are sometimes so afraid of contami-
nating the rigorous methods of pure science with the looser, less
accurate methods which prevail in the practical or applied fields that
our greatest experimentalist, Michelson, dropped all his researches in
radioactivity when he learnt that it had practical medical applications.
This was due not to any hatred of human welfare, but rather to an
honorable conviction that the love of truth, like the love of beauty
is its own excuse for being, and does not need the justification that it
is ministerial to something else which may be of lesser inherent or
intrinsic value.

I do not wish to overstate this point. It is true that some problems
of physics have suggested fruitful researches in pure mathematics,
and progress in theoretic physics has sometimes resulted from attempts
to solve problems of technology. But the dangers to science from too
great preoccupation with practical results are much greater in a social
than in the physical realm. Erroneous physical generalizations are
likely sooner or later to be contradicted by readily observable physical

phenomena about which there can be little difference of opinion. Thus the Ptolemaic astronomy is contradicted by the observable phases of Venus, and Newton's corpuscular theory of light by the observable results in Young's and Fresnel's experiments. But we cannot so readily eliminate false hypotheses in the social realm. In the first place, men, women and social groups do not as readily submit to laboratory experiments as do inanimate objects or helpless fruit flies and guinea pigs. Even if we take the whole of history as our laboratory, it is not always possible to decide on objective ground such relatively simple questions as which kind of government works better. Democracy, hereditary monarchy and dictatorships have been repeatedly tried and are still being tried. What is the objective lesson of experience? If you believe in democracy, the consequences of dictatorship seem horrible. But if you believe in fascism, the consequences seem much better than those of democracy. The same objective fact thus proves different things to men who approach it with different ideas. The notion that we can study social facts apart from any assumption or working hypothesis has been repeatedly shown to be logically fantastic.

It may be urged that whatever we believe, social conduct is still governed, like the rest of nature by determined laws. This dogmatic assumption, however, will not help us much, and Professor Robinson himself does not assume that beliefs affect our acts. But waiving this point, we may well consider the suggestion that even if social conduct is governed by determinate laws, all that we know tends to indicate that if there are any invariant natural laws of social behavior, they are so much more complicated than the laws of biology, and of inorganic physics, that there is little likelihood of our ever being able to discover them or to manipulate them. We can deal with equations which formulate such laws only if they contain a limited number of variables, but the number of variables in the social field may for a long time be too large for our power of comparison. Indeed, even in the physical realm there are regions which for this reason continue to baffle us, so that we cannot find the laws or patterns which determine the phenomena therein.

If Professor Robinson's positive assertions as to what psychology now offers to legal science have thus to be viewed with caution, his negative assertions are even less promising. The need of liberalism in science and practice makes it necessary to be on guard against his and other obstinate efforts to ignore or confuse the distinction between the law that is established and the law that ought to be.

Of course, in practice he must and does assume that many actually existing laws work badly or unjustly and ought not to be the law. Indeed, a large part of the book is devoted to this theme. But his uncritical view of ethics and his narrow or near-sighted naturalism prevent him from forming a clear conception of the difference between considerations as to what does exist and considerations as to what ought to exist. He misapprehends the issue even when he quotes Pound and others who have made that distinction, and supposes it to be whether increased knowledge can modify our moral evaluation in specific instances. But that is something which the writers quoted in no way deny. The application of an ethical or any other principle to any situation must be based on assumptions as to the facts of the case, and any change in such assumptions will necessarily change the conclusion. The real issue is not whether factual knowledge is necessary for a moral judgment but whether it is sufficient without a distinctly ethical premise. Can we from a number of premises which describe what *is* deduce a conclusion which prescribes what *ought to be?* Reflection shows this to be logically impossible and morally confusing. Can we, e.g., derive from the merely natural or factual knowledge of physiology and hygiene the duty to preserve our health? Professor Robinson seems to assume that we can. But reflection shows this to be indefensible dogmatism. We may know as much physiology or hygiene as any physician does and yet not be more rationally persuaded than physicians generally are that it is our duty to preserve our health in all circumstances. We may prefer to sacrifice it for wealth, power, beauty, the safety of our children, or of our country, or to preserve our moral integrity. And if any natural scientist should call the exercise of such preference foolish or irrational, we should tell him that he is not minding his own business, and that the gentle art of applying derogatory epithets is no part of natural science.[2]

The fact is that those who think that they can deal with the facts of social life without making any judgments of what ought to be,

---

[2] Professor Robinson objects to the statement that over and above the factual judgments of descriptive social science we need those of legal science, of what the law demands. He might with equal propriety object to a physicist saying that over and above the determination of geometry we need the assumption of time to get kinematics, and, over and above the latter, the assumption of forces to get dynamics.

simply ignore the ethical assumptions implicit in or necessary to their actual arguments, just as our courts often think that they are stating the law without any economic theories when in fact they are relying on ancient economic assumptions which they happen not to have ever questioned. Similarly, we find jurists like Duguit announcing that they are concerned only with the law that is and yet ending with a conclusion that certain proposed reforms *ought not* to be accepted. They do that because they smuggle in some assumption as to what is desirable or ought to be—generally a preference for the status quo. But in ethics as in natural science an assumption is no better or truer because it is unavowed and has not been submitted to critical examination.

Professor Robinson is therefore mistaken in identifying ethics with the defense of traditional moral judgments—though unfortunately many writers in ethics are preachers of traditional morality. As a critique of moral judgments ethics is a liberating exercise of our intelligence. By showing that not only traditional but some reformatory moral judgments are often untenable as inconsistent, confused or really meaningless, we liberate ourselves from blind dogmatism and become more tolerant of diversity.

In the light of the foregoing considerations we need not take very seriously Professor Robinson's two efforts to break down the distinction between what *is* and what *ought to be*. The first is an attempt to identify the law that *ought to be* with the law that *is coming to be,* i.e., with the future. That is obviously false if we remember that bad or unjust laws which ought not to be created by legislatures and courts may be *coming to be* in the future as they have *come to be* in the past. Indeed, if we take Professor Robinson literally then, since every existing law has ceased to be something in the future, it has ceased to be that which is good or ought to be. Every existing law then is unjust—a curious result from a realist who is also not an anarchist.

Not altogether unaware of the difficulties in which this distinction involves him, Professor Robinson tries to wipe it out entirely by contending that all judgments, whether in regard to existence or value, are as such psychologic facts. It is however obviously fallacious to argue that such an identity can wipe out an important difference. The fact that winter and summer are both seasons, cannot deny the vital difference between them.

Professor Robinson's opposition to explicitly ethical considerations seems based, partly at least, on the narrow positivist or naturalistic view which restricts science to the study of what actually exists. This, however, is quite erroneous. It is impossible to so restrict mathematics, rational dynamics, or indeed, any other theoretic science; for these deal rather with abstractions or what would exist under certain circumstances, some of which are actually impossible, e.g., the laws of falling bodies in a perfect vacuum. Indeed, in this very book we have the recognition of a psychologic problem that deals with an abstract deliberation that cannot by itself occur in nature. (P. 170.)

It must be admitted that in the field of ethics there has prevailed a great diversity of views which is likely to continue. But this does not mean that ethical judgments are not capable of being rationally organized into a coherent or rigorously logical system. This involves not only knowledge of natural causal relations which determine what means are necessary for certain ends, but also a critical consideration of what is ultimately good or worth while and for which we ought to strive. Such a system may be called a rational art rather than science. We need not be concerned about the name provided we remember that all theoretic sciences are rational arts and contain dialectic or deductive elements, that ethical considerations cannot in fact be eliminated completely from any of the social sciences, and that ethical judgments can be verified if applied to long spans of human experience, though much verification because of its subject matter cannot be as relatively simple as it is in the natural sciences. The question then is not whether we shall or shall not allow ethical considerations to enter into the study of law, but whether our ethics shall be made explicit and critically examined, or unavowed and blindly dogmatic. The refusal to recognize the distinction between what is and what ought to be naturally leads to the assumption that what is, is right, which Professor Robinson himself recognizes in practice to be fatal to progress, to the effort to achieve our heart's desire.

Intellectual humility on the part of those who seek the truth is not only a grace but a necessity; and it is well that legal scholars in this country should show a willingness to learn from all possible sources. But it is also necessary to be on guard against the easy assumption that any proposition becomes true when someone labels it natural science. Science should surely not be another name for credulity.

CHAPTER TEN

The Rational Basis of Legal Institutions

I F REVIEWING books were the judicial function that it ought to be, I should be disqualified in this case. For as a member of the editorial committee of the Legal Philosophy Series my advice as to the making of this book was asked and in some cases followed. But as some of the notices of this book have been rather unjust in failing to take account of what the editors actually set out to do, a review from the latter point of view may be worth while.

The book is based on the assumption that it is very important that we should consider the reason or justification for the fundamental legal institutions. Put baldly in this way, our assumption may sound like a truism the insistence on which can hardly seem necessary at a time when there is an apparently general acceptance of the idea that law is to be studied scientifically at a university and not as a mere trade at a trade school. But in fact, we have two parties in opposition to the idea that the reason of the law is of any importance. In the first place there are the old-fashioned conservatives, who hold that the law is a closed body of rules—rules so definite that there is no use in theoretic discussion about them, since such discussion cannot change them. But neither history nor logic bears out this view. We know that the law has been constantly, if slowly, changing and that the reasons which judges and jurists have given for various legal rules have influenced the subsequent development (by the process of interpretation) of these rules. The *reasons* found in the Federalist or those given by John Marshall in *Marbury v. Madison* or in *McCulloch v. Maryland* have certainly been a determining factor in the subsequent development of our constitutional law. The same people who assert that law is law and has nothing to do with theory, generally rely confidently on such dogmas as that that government is best which governs least. This and a host of other illustrations which will readily occur

A review of *The Rational Basis of Legal Institutions* in *Yale Law Journal,* Vol. 33, p. 892 (1924). Reprinted by permission of the publisher.

to any student of legal history would make the conservative's position untenable, if he were not, in his contempt for reason, reenforced (as conservatives generally are) by those who regard themselves as radicals, such as Marxians, positivists, behaviorists, and psycho-analysts. All these, while differing markedly among each other as to the causes of legal development, are united in the dogma that the reasons we give for any legal institution cannot possibly have any effective influence on its growth or administration. But without denying that economic and organic motives have their place in the law as in other fields of social life, it is rather easy to show that the dogmatic denial of all influence to reason, the idea that we can keep on professing certain reasons without having them exert any influence, is just a snap judgment unsupported by serious evidence from the realm of law and in fact inconsistent with the profession of trying to improve its practice by better scientific teaching. For better or for worse the reason or justification for the law of property, contract, etc., is under discussion in the community at large; and the lawyer cannot ignore this or take the position that all discussion is absolutely futile. He must appeal to general principles in his defence of what he considers the legitimate interests of property, personality, etc. By reasoning also we transform the law from an endless catalogue of bare rules, remembered by rote, into a coherent system deducible from principles and therefore more flexible and more easily adjustable to novel situations.

If the foregoing considerations have any merit, they show the necessity not only for general theory or philosophy of law, but more especially for books which will acquaint students with the different influential views which have been actually held as to the rational justification (or condemnation) of the various fundamental legal institutions. To determine whether these reasons are sound or not will of course involve knowledge of history, as well as of contemporary social fact. But neither legal history nor contemporary social information can eliminate the necessity of a juristic analysis of the fundamental aims at the basis of the different legal institutions. Such an analysis is not only necessary to determine to what extent the law renders the service claimed for it, but also necessary for any coherent or truly scientific development of the law that exists. Indispensable as is a general textbook of the type of Dean Pound's "Introduction to Legal Philosophy," there is need also of a source-book which should give the different views as to the rationale of legal institutions in the words of their original or most powerful proponents, and should follow as far as possible the manner in which the law is generally split up in our law schools into a number of subjects such as persons, contracts, civil wrongs, property, crime, procedure, etc.

This volume then is to be judged primarily as an effort at a new type of text for students of law, occupying an intermediate position between the ordinary case-books and treatises on the general theory of law. It shares with the latter the aim of building up a general background against which the perspectives of various legal rules can be more justly estimated; but it shares with the casebook the pedagogic advantage of offering no ready solutions but compelling the student to weigh for himself the different contentions.

As to the manner in which Messrs. Wigmore and Kocourek have executed their task it is very easy to be censorious—in fact too easy, since we are involved here in matters of judgment on which a wide diversity of opinion is possible. Thus many selections seem to me perfectly valueless, containing nothing but commonplace opinions dressed up in starched sociologic terminology. But possibly they are for that reason all the more valuable, as being perfect specimens of their kind, so plentiful nowadays. In any case I have no confidence that many more would agree with my own selection from the enormous literature of this field. I venture to think, however, that many of the needless repetitions in this volume could well have been omitted to make room for appropriate extracts from judicial decisions and other legal authorities to illustrate the way in which general social conceptions do in fact enter into the matter of strictly legal issues. Even more confident am I that it is an error to leave out the rationale of the institution of legal personality, and, even more so, of legal procedure. The logic of mathematical and physical science has made great progress by realizing that many fundamental principles or axioms are really rules of procedure, and similar progress in legal science will be blocked by too sharp a separation between substantive law and procedure.

Almost all the selections on property—which fill nearly half of the volume—illustrate what philosophers call the fallacy of vicious abstraction. Property is discussed as if it were just one simple thing existing by itself. In view of the fact that almost everyone believes both (1) in some amount of government or limitation on the right of individuals to do as they please, and (2) in some sphere of individual freedom to dispose of things in accordance with our pleasure, the significant question is not whether you are for or against private property, but rather where you will draw the line between public and private things and affairs. May there be private property in human beings (slavery), in public office, in the immoral use of things (intoxicants, etc.)? How far may a state expropriate an industry by entering into competition with it, or how far may it use the power of taxation to discourage undesirable enterprises? Questions of this sort are really more significant as to the meaning of private property than abstract arguments such as the one (p. 189) that private property is a guarantee of the desire for possession. For obviously the institution of private property is also a thwarting of this desire on the part of all who are not legal possessors. Indeed modern ownership of capital really amounts to a right to tax those who wish to use certain tools. This tax may be for the good of all in the long run, but the argument that such a system sets examples of thrift sounds too ironic (p. 366). Another type of argument which is singularly inconclusive is the one used by Mr. Paul Elmer More to the effect that private property despite its cruelty is necessary to our civilization. It might be replied that it begs the question as to whether a civilization that allows certain cruel injustices is worth preserving.

Indeed, the overpowering impression which the reading of this book makes on one interested in sound thinking, is the awful amount of nonsense written by worthy people on serious and momentous subjects. The very first selection, from Spencer, is based on a patent confusion between "law of nature" as a uniformity of existence and "law of nature" as a norm of what ought to be. Obviously, if laws of nature are absolute uniformities we cannot possible violate them or act contrary to them, and to condemn certain legislation as an interference with them (pp. 4ff.) is absolute nonsense. Though this confusion has been repeatedly pointed out by Huxley, Pearson and others, it continues to dominate popular thought. Nor is the laboriously conscientious Mill free from this confusion between what is and what ought to be (p. 16, end of sec. 2). But it is unnecessary to multiply examples. All absolute statements such as Mill's "The despotism of custom is everywhere the standing hindrance to human advancement," can be met by showing the equal truth of the contrary, e.g.: All human advancement depends on the mechanism of habit or custom." It is only when through accurate factual knowledge we can reduce our statements to precise quantitative form, that any proposition about social life becomes more true than its contrary. So long as this is the case it behooves us to approach all these questions with profound humility and tolerance.

Meanwhile let us be thankful for a volume which contains such splendid and illuminating essays as those of Roscoe Pound, L. K. McMurray, and Charmont.

CHAPTER ELEVEN

American Interpretations of Natural Law

T HIS BOOK is the expansion of a doctoral dissertation and, like other works of this type, it shows greater regard for fullness of documentation than for the illumination of fundamental ideas. Following the work of Merriam, Gettell, and Haines, Professor Wright has read and abstracted many pamphlets, printed speeches, and some treatises in which the concept of natural law is explicitly or implicitly used. The result is a useful compilation of sources, important and unimportant, as to the colonial, revolutionary and pre-civil-war periods, with fewer but clearer references to later writers. Professor Wright does not seem to have any first hand familiarity with our juristic literature and modestly admits that "the portion of Chapter IX which deals with judicial opinions is essentially a shorter and more superficial survey of material dealt with by Prof. Haines in his Revival of Natural Law Concepts." It is, therefore, not surprising that he fails to get the point of *Gitlow v. New York* (pp. 304-305). However, he does show that James Wilson, Chase, Marshall, Story, Kent, Cooley and Miller were all of the opinion that courts have the right to set aside legislative enactments as against natural law even where there is no violation of any specific provision of the Constitution; and if this is no longer so often asserted, it is because the same result is now achieved by stretching the fifth and fourteenth amendments to the Constitution and the requirement of "due process."

The last chapter gives a brief summary of the history of the American use of the concept of natural law in its various meanings and concludes with an attempt to indicate its permanent significance. The distinction between natural law as a description of an *existing* order and as a prescription of what *ought to be* is well drawn and the confusion resulting from trying to derive one from the other is aptly pointed out. But the difficulties of making law conform to justice do

A review of *American Interpretations of Natural Law* by Benjamin F. Wright in *Yale Law Journal*, Vol. 41, p. 1102 (1932). Reprinted by permission of the publisher.

not justify the conclusion that it is an "attempt to solve the insolvable." (p. 345).

Professor Wright disarms criticism of his book by his modest disclaimer of any "careful estimate of the relative position of the concept of natural law in the entire body of American political thought." That, he thinks, is one of "the things which can be done only after many additional studies in this field have been made." (p. ix). That may be so. But the requisite additional studies need not be directed solely to the further unearthing of deservedly forgotten writers. Not all who wrote long ago are important any more than all who write today. Many who have written have had little, if any, influence, and it is not necessary to follow every straw to see the direction of a current. It is, however, important to trace the actual history of the great current of thought on natural law. Those who do so will find that Puritan thought in America was not autonomous, but rather an offshoot of Puritan thought in England, which was Calvinistic in origin. Professor Wright would have done well if he had distinguished between the Protestant and the Catholic doctrines of natural law. Catholic writers have used the concept of natural law to defend the right of members of the Church to disobey certain enactments of temporal sovereigns (which explains the position of Father Ryan in the note on p. 276), while Protestant thinkers like Grotius and Hobbes, tried to liberate the State (which claimed dominion over the national church) from the rule of the Roman Pontiff. With the rapid expansion of modern commerce and industry the 18th century doctrines of natural law began to emphasize the rights of the individual man, and especially of the business man, against the rulers of the state. And it was this view that vitalized the thought of the French, as well as of the American Revolution. Ultimately, then, the essence of all doctrines of natural rights is the view that any established or proposed social order or institution must defend itself before the bar of human welfare. In this sense the doctrine has not only a great past but is significant for today and for tomorrow.

CHAPTER TWELVE

A French View of Jurisprudence

T HIS BOOK is the outcome of an introductory course of the kind
often given in continental law schools to orient the student as to
the human implications of the law. In accordance with recent tendencies among French writers—witness Geny, Renard, Hauriou, Le Fur,
Rippert, and even Duguit—more than three quarters of this substantial
volume is devoted to the normative aspect of the legal order. This does
not mean that Dabin confuses law and morality. On the contrary, the
distinction between them is perhaps too sharply drawn. But he
rightly insists that it is theoretically and practically dangerous to ignore,
as the positivists do, what the law ought to be, as it is dangerous
to ignore, with some moralists, that law is law even when not moral
or just.

In the introductory section, positive law is distinguished from morality by the fact that the former is definitely determined and sanctioned
by a specific social authority. This is connected with a difference of
aim. The law seeks the common or public good by regulating the
social relations between individuals, while morality is concerned with
the whole human good of the individual person. Legal rules are thus
not mere phenomena of existence, but they involve also the question
of the legitimacy of the authority which posits them and the evaluation of the aims and results of such rules. The enforcement of the
law generally depends upon a certain amount of respect for it, so that
actual physical constraint is not always necessary.

Section I deals with the conditions of positive law. The author rejects as inadequate the positivistic account of law as a body of rules
that happen to prevail. He puts himself in the position of the judge
or jurist who has to decide what is the proper legal rule in a given
situation. Decisions in such cases can not be entirely arbitrary if the
law is to operate at all. Some regard for the common good must control. The point is well made that while the prevailing public opinion

A review of *La Philosophie de l'Ordre Juridique Positif, Specialement dans
Les Rapports de Droit Privé* by Jean Dabin in *Yale Law Journal*, Vol. 40,
p. 1336 (1931). Reprinted by permission of the publisher.

controls the general aim of the law, the specific rules must be elaborated by trained jurists. Not everything we want can be formed into legal rules. Our various ends must be mutually coherent if they are to enter the legal order, and this can be effected only through attention to the objective order of our material. A logically coherent body of law is also more readily known and serves better the social need of security. This means that many things morally indifferent in themselves must be made legally determinate.

The second section is devoted to a discussion of natural law, justice and Catholic Christian morality in relation to the legal order. Natural law is a definite part of the moral law, that part indeed which can be enforced as distinguished from such moral rules as that of charity or purity of heart. Dabin's conception of natural law is that of Aristotle and St. Thomas. He has little respect for the seventeenth and eighteenth century variety which was an idealized picture of Roman law. The upholders of this view did not consistently seek for first principles of what the law should be, but pretended to find a complete system of detailed legal rules that should be in force everywhere at all times. They did not allow for the variations of human nature and social conditions. This in part led to the positivistic effort to describe the law that *is* without reference to what it ought to be. This effort, however, cannot succeed. It leads only to unavowed natural law principles. Adhering, as Dabin does, to the Aristotelian distinction between form and matter, he defends Stammler's view of natural law with variable content. He does not, however, do justice to Stammler because knowing him only indirectly (mainly through Geny), he does not grasp the German distinction between *Moralität* and *Sittlichkeit*.

In his conception of justice Dabin follows Tourtoulon and others in confining it to the maxim *suum cuique tribuere* without fully allowing for the fact that what we regard as a man's own is largely the product of our legal order. As a result of this narrow conception it becomes possible to assert that the public good often demands things in conflict with justice — which is not true on a wider conception of it. He may, however, conceive of justice as a necessary though not sufficient condition of public welfare. The latter requires positive measures of sanitation, of safe-guarding the human and natural resources of the community and the like — all of which pass beyond the negative requirements of mere justice. But this necessitates the introduction of positive moral rules into the legal order. To the ordinary objection that such moral rules are too variable, Dabin contends that if we take Catholic Christian morality we find its aims more definite and stable than those of the legal order. This is a large and controversial issue. But any discussion of it must draw a clearer line than Dabin himself does between the invariant principle of morality and the specific moral rules which are to fit the changing conditions of human life.

In the third section we have the application of moral principles to specific legal issues. Given the facts of our psychologic constitution, our economic system and our family and political organization, what limits must be imposed on our moral principles to produce desirable legal results? Keen arguments are presented to show why the interests of social security and the limitations of legal procedure prevent us from correcting all unfair advantages in contracts, why continued possession should give title, and why one may be held responsible for the damage caused by another. These arguments, however, are in part rendered necessary only by an uncritical and narrow conception of justice. The latter also leads Professor Dabin to fallacious economic arguments to prove that a manufacturer derives extra benefits from the fact that his workmen have children, so that he may justly be compelled to pay such workmen higher wages. If the community desires more children, or better income for larger families, it must face the problem more directly.

The fourth section deals in the main with the problem of unjust law. Here Dabin takes a wider view of the term justice and rejects social welfare as too vague a criterion of the difference between just and unjust law. He insists that the latter term is to be applied to any enactment or rule that conflicts with our religious or moral duty. He duly emphasizes the fact that the social security protected by the legal order serves the larger human good and that therefore disobedience of law is likely to produce greater harm than that generally wrought by bad laws. Yet Dabin faces more honestly than most writers on jurisprudence the obvious truth that laws often have bad moral effects and are oppressive and narrowly partisan. While positivists are right in insisting that there can be no *legal* right of resistance to the law, they ignore the fact that in conscience the whole legal system rests on its claim to serve the common good. There must come a point, then, at which resistance, passive or active, is justified. The danger of destroying the legal order is not to be regarded lightly. But in the end no human institution can claim absolute perfection, and the law, like the Sabbath, being made for man, must be broken when it stands in the way of his greater good.

As might be expected from an introductory treatise, this book discusses elementary issues with due and earnest regard for formal completeness and precision. It lacks the terseness that one used to expect of neo-scholastic literature, and which is unfortunately becoming rare among French legal writers. The book is heavily documented, but only from French sources that treat the same subject. The obvious narrowness of the outlook is, however, compensated by a certain refreshingly simple sincerity. For readers in our own country it is instructive in showing that while some of our own advanced law teachers are becoming positivistic (in reaction against narrow legal fundamentalism) the current of European scholarship is abandoning that position and realizing more that the life of the law is in its aim and the way it serves a just ideal of communal life. The narrowly practical lawyer may view the law as merely our predictions of the rules which the courts will follow. But this is like viewing medicine as our prediction of what the physicians will prescribe. One who wishes for a better understanding must view the law in the making and take account of the considerations which should lead the judge or jurist to decide which of a number of conflicting rules best serves the purpose of a legal order. We cannot well dispense with a consideration of the reason and purpose of the law.

CHAPTER THIRTEEN

A Glimpse of Colonial Law

NOT MANY years ago the Dean of one of our leading law schools used to address his class as follows: "If you want to be a 'nut,' read Pollock and Maitland but if you want to know the law of New York State, read the cases." Great progress has since then taken place in our law schools and the prestige of Maitland's humane scholarship is now very high indeed. Still, his influence, even in England, is largely restricted to the study of medieval land law, the field wherein worked Littleton, Coke and Spellman. The history of more modern industrial and commercial law is still relatively a neglected province. Legal scholarship therefore owes a great debt to Professor Morris and to Professor Goebel for their pioneer work on American colonial law, which bids fair to throw light not only on our own but also on English legal history.

The present volume is the second in a series of American legal records under the auspices of the American Historical Association. It contains minutes of the Mayor's Court from 1674, when the English rule was reestablished, to 1784 when American independence was established in New York City. For a few of the cases there are extracts from the papers containing the pleading. There are over 300 cases, covering almost every phase of law, with generous allowance for commercial and admiralty law. Professor Morris' Introduction gives an admirable account of the origin of the Mayor's Court in London, the extent of its jurisdiction and the way in which the Mayor's Court of New York City followed it. As between those who, like Judge Daly, magnify the Dutch influence and those who, like Professor Goebel, tend to minimize it, Professor Morris holds an intermediate position. Professor Morris also gives us some valuable information about the personnel of the bench and the bar of the Mayor's Court.

I have found the volume fascinating reading because of the direct way in which it reflects colonial life in New York City, its gossip and

A review of *Select Cases of the Mayor's Court of New York City, 1674-1784,* edited by Richard B. Morris in *Columbia Law Review,* Vol. 36, p. 1388 (1936). Reprinted by permission of the publisher.

back-biting as well as its way of doing business. It is instructive to read of the plight of children apprenticed and running back to their homes because they were not adequately fed or clothed and too freely beaten. Eloquent of the administration of colonial criminal law is the case of Bauman, guilty of stealing "a mulatto slave and a cannon," sentenced to receive 39 stripes at the whipping post and afterwards to be returned to his master as indentured servant for five years and six months more in consideration of the damage to Mr. Smith. On the whole, however, one leaves the volume with the impression of rather high legal competence on the part of the judges, even though there seems to have been no systematic provision for legal education within the apprentice system.

I should like to take issue with Professor Morris in regard to his comments on *Rutgers v. Waddington*. Professor Morris sees in this case an anticipation of "judicial review" and says that it is clear from this case and several others in the critical period that the argument for judicial review had already been "well aired in the State courts." If judicial review means the power of the court to set aside a statute as contrary to the state constitution, there is not a word of such a claim in the case. On the contrary, the court professes to follow the statute but to give it an equitable interpretation. Of course, the case might well have been decided on the ground that under the Articles of Confederation a treaty of the United States took precedence over a previously enacted state law; and something of this may be said to be floating in the opinion of the court. But even so there is an obvious difference between such subordination of a state to the Union of which it is a part and judicial review as a power of a state court to declare a legislative act void as a violation of the state constitution or the power of a federal court to set aside an act of the other two coordinate branches of the government. What is really significant about *Rutgers v. Waddington* is the illustration of the fact that the ideas distinguishing public law from morality were not at that time sharply formulated. The quotations from Grotius, Vattel, and Burlamaqui all move in the twilight zone between law and ethics. It was in this twilight zone that the doctrine of the power of the courts to set aside legislative enactments had its origin.

CHAPTER FOURTEEN

Law and Civilization

D R. ROBSON is a distinguished barrister and Reader in Administrative Law in the University of London, who has recently discovered the seminal fact that law is part of human life and, like the rest of it, influenced by men's ideas about nature in general. This discovery has suggested to him a liberal and interesting course of reading in rather familiar and for the most part secondary sources. Though we are assured that "the essential aim throughout has been to present a synthesis," the result looks more like the elaboration of a student's notebook than like an original systematic work on the subject. There is a noticeable lack of a clear and coherent set of ideas to hold together the diverse observations and bits of information. In the end it is not even clear what our author means by *law* and how it differs from custom.

Part I, entitled The Origins of Law, is in the main devoted to illustrations of the influence of supernatural ideas and practices on legal and political institutions. These illustrations are generally suggestive and sometimes illuminating, especially in the chapter on Curses, Blessings, Oaths. Students, however, should be warned against the methodologic frailties of books of this sort. In the first place, one must be on guard against the great vice of popular anthropology, so strikingly represented by J. G. Frazier, to wit, building on reports of others without the most rudimentary critical examination of their competence or reliability. Even when the authorities are of the most unexceptional character, one is apt to misapprehend what they say and fall into serious error if he is not himself familiar with the subject matter. This is illustrated by Dr. Robson's remark that Kepler's laws mark the first occasion when laws of nature were expressed in mathematical terms (shades of Archimedes!), or by his attributing to the Greeks the view that human life is a reign of law but that Nature is chaos. Even more serious, however, because more subtle, is the error of what

A review of *Civilization and the Growth of Law*, by William A. Robson in *Harvard Law Review*, 145 (1936). Reprinted by permission of the publisher.

may be called the anecdotal method, according to which illustrations are drawn from the ideas and customs of the most diverse people without regard to their actual historical background and meaning. This method vitiates the work even of men of genius like Montesquieu and renders scientifically worthless such generalizations as those of Herbert Spencer. On the whole it results in overemphasizing the bizarre in the customs of ancient and primitive people to the neglect of the common human elements which make these customs comprehensible in terms of our own daily experience.

Part II is entitled The Law of Nature and goes over the rather familiar field of discussion of natural rights, natural law, and the state of nature. Dr. Robson unfortunately has not a firm grip on the history of this theme. He clearly misses some of the most significant points in the work of Grotius.

In Part III, entitled The Nature of Law, the author proposes "to survey and analyse the relationship existing between contemporary science and contemporary law." What Dr. Robson actually does, however, is to try to show that we can "reunite natural law with the laws of man by acknowledging the legislative power and creative ability of the human intellect to be the source of both." Now this philosophic idealism may be what Eddington and some other eminent scientists have said in their popular works, but it is as illegitimate to identify contemporary science with this view, as with the views of any religious denomination or political party which counts some distinguished scientists among its members. It is well to heed what distinguished men say on subjects of their special competence, but the opinions of a mathematical physicist on philosophy, education, morals or politics are not science. If we disregard what men of science say when in the pulpit and watch what they do when they are engaged in physical investigation or mathematical computation, we find them invariably taking for granted what geological evidence makes explicit, viz., that there was a material world before man and his legislative activity ever came on the scene. It is flattering to human vanity to make man the creator of nature or its laws, but if we were to take this seriously, we should have to say that we also create our own ancestors and the biologic laws according to which we have come into this world.

The hazy idealism which ignores such obvious facts has no difficulty in ignoring the existence of police, sheriffs, militia, jails, prisons, and other agencies concerned with penalties for those who disobey legal commands. Law doubtless involves more than brute force, and Dr. Robson would be on firm ground if he were satisfied to note how frequently law evolves a generally convenient pattern of conduct. But every law necessarily affects some class of persons differently from others. Hence no government can exist without some force to compel obedience to its commands. Dr. Robson adds only vehemence but not logical force to the many vain attempts to overthrow this sound core in Austin's theory of law.

Altogether the spirit of this book is that of humane liberalism, but also of pious disinclination to come to close grips intellectually with the hard realities of law, realities that are inseparable from the human lack of omniscience, omnipotence and universal good will.

Index of Names

Index of Subjects